Stone the Builders Rejected

By
Johnnie Goolsby

*Foreword by Joy Freeman and
Pastor Pamela Y. Payne*

Edited by Deborah E. Fraley

xulon PRESS

Copyright © 2002 by Johnnie Goolsby

Stone the Builders Rejected
by Johnnie Goolsby

Printed in the United States of America

Library of Congress Control Number: 2002104933
ISBN 1-591600-66-9

All rights reserved. No part of this publication may be reproduced or transmitted in any form or by any means without written permission of the publisher.

Unless otherwise indicated, Bible quotations are taken from the King James Version of the Bible.

Back Cover photograph courtesy of Horace Holmes Photography Studios, Macon, Ga.
(www.HoraceHolmesStudio.com)

Xulon Press
11350 Random Hills Road
Suite 800
Fairfax, VA 22030
(703) 279-6511
XulonPress.com

To order additional copies, call 1-866-909-BOOK (2665).

Donated by...

Johnnie Goolsby
January 15, 2004

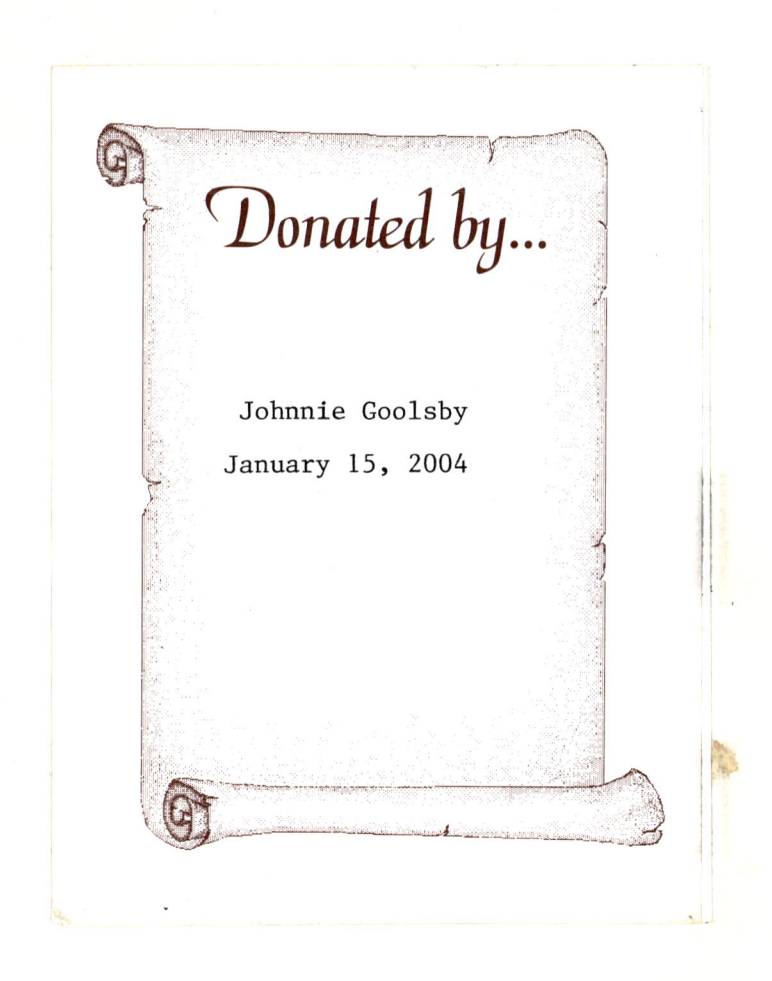

MONROE COUNTY LIBRARY
FORSYTH, GEORGIA

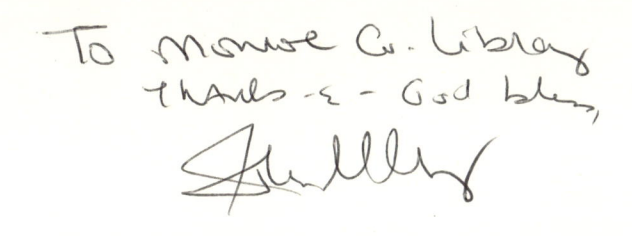

Dedication

∞

To my family…
To my first love…
Jesus

Foreword

∞

One of the greatest blessings that God can give someone is a friend that has all of the qualities that defines one as a friend. Johnnie has been that great blessing. Seldom does anyone encounter a person with such rare and refreshing qualities as she has. I had the pleasure of working with her for several years and that is how our relationship began. Since that time we have become close and are prayer partners. Her commitment and dedication to the Lord is exceptional. She faces the challenges of this day with grace, determination, and perseverance. I know that she is dedicated to her family, and that her life is a living testimony to all who have the good fortune of knowing her. I have faced some very discouraging and trying circumstances in my life. I do not believe that I could have made it through without all the prayers, calls, words of wisdom, and encouragement that I received from her.

I admire Johnnie for waiting on the Lord for a Godly mate. She has kept herself pure for the man that God has waiting for her. I know that she was placed in the kingdom for such a time as this and I thank God every day that I too, am here to share this time with her. The effectual prayer of a righteous man availeth much and I know that Johnnie has that kind of prayer life. She is a rare and precious jewel that has made my life richer.

—Joy Freeman

Johnnie Goolsby has been a friend of mine for many years and I have always admired and appreciated her stand on abstinence and other moral issues. Her faith in God has brought her through the fiery trials of life's circumstances. I have seen her grow in strength and faith.

She was always firm in her beliefs and doing what she felt the Lord would have her to do. Through her college years, I saw her persevere in her education, personal, and spiritual life. Ms. Goolsby has gained a wealth of knowledge through learning and life experiences. Her love for others is shown through the many years of working with the elderly and now with young adults.

She never gives up and this is exhibited through her many achievements. By overcoming many obstacles in life, she is truly a living testimony of what God is able to do when He is first in our lives. She is an inspiration to many because she chose to conquer the enemy through the Word of God. I have always found her to be a person of remarkable integrity and honor, possessing unconditional love for all of mankind. I am thrilled that she is making a remarkable impact through young adults with her ministry. Many young people are realizing that they do not have to give in to peer pressure, but can stand for Godly principles and keep their temples holy unto Our Father.

Johnnie is the epitome of a virtuous woman…

―—Pastor Pamela Y. Payne
Fruit of the Spirit Ministries

Introduction

Abstinence is a topic that is not discussed enough. It is time for the body of Christ to stand up and become more vocal on the issues that Jesus Christ embraced. Sexual purity is one of those issues. This book encourages us to have respect for our bodies. It's about keeping our temples pure emotionally, physically, and spiritually in order to serve the Lord at maximum capacity! It's about putting the pressure of our peers behind us. It's about standing on the Word of God, and refusing to give it up, no matter what the cost.

Abstinence is really speaking into the lives of people today…

The sweetest gift one can give to their new spouse is the gift of purity. It is also an order from God. He knew the problems we'd have if we didn't keep His commandments. Problems of dealing with ex-mates, child support, and sexually transmitted diseases were never in God's plan. My greatest wish is for my child's life to be prosperous in every area of her life. Therefore, I speak freely to my eleven year-old regarding sexual abstinence and all the wonderful blessings God provides when she keeps His commandments. Yes, I truly believe abstinence "makes the heart grow fonder"…

—Carolyn Randall

As a woman and mother, I feel that abstinence should be one of the greatest blessings a young woman can possess because you can keep your self-respect and control your destiny. In doing this, the Lord will send you the right person to spend your life with…

—Margaret Brown

I pray that this book will reveal that the gift of abstinence until marriage is the sweetest blessing a couple can share on their wedding night.

And now I present to you…*Stone the Builders Rejected.*

Table of Contents

∞

Dedication..v
Foreword...vii
Introduction ix

1. Presenting a Beautiful Body in the Eyes of God
   Romans 12:1-2 13

2. The Revelation
   Isaiah 55:10-11...19

3. Because of the Love of the Father
   Colossians 3:20 25

4. Following the Master
   Matthew 9:9 29

5. Listening to His Voice
   Matthew 11:28-30 33

6. Hope Grows Dim
   Psalm 26:1-3 39

7. The Final Shattered Plan
   Luke 6:45 43

8. Pain Exposed in the Presence of a Loving God
   Luke 6:46-49 51

9. Facing the Cross, Despising My Sin
   Matthew 16:24-25 59

10. Choosing for the Cause of Christ
    Luke 16:13 67

11. Definition of a Miracle
    John 5:5-9...71

12. How Bad Do You Really Want It?
    Matthew 13:1-9 81

13. Is It Worth the Wait?
    Matthew 13:44-46 87

14. Behold...A Handmaiden of the Lord!
    Luke 20:17-18 93

1

Presenting a Beautiful Body in the Eyes of God

∞

> I beseech you therefore, brethren, by the mercies of God, that ye present your bodies a living sacrifice, holy, acceptable unto God, which is your reasonable service. And be not conformed to this world: but be ye transformed by the renewing of your mind, that ye may prove what is that good, and acceptable, and perfect will of God.
> *Romans 12:1-2*

God does not condone sexual promiscuity. He makes it very clear throughout the Bible that we should remain sexually abstinent until marriage. He wants our bodies to be as pure temples in order to bring Him glory. For some people, however, this can become a difficult pill to swallow. Making such a decision requires self-sacrifice, extreme discipline, and an undying love and allegiance to Jesus Christ. We must be able to withstand criticism, turmoil, and harassment from the demonic forces of the world that operate through humans. It compels us to take up our crosses daily, not to be seen by men, but because we love the Lord more than self.

Everyone that sets out on such a journey will not make it. But those that are willing to take the course that leads to a beautiful and deeply intimate relationship with Jesus will always be happy that they did.

There are still people in this generation who are virgins and have made a commitment to be sexually abstinent until they get married. There are also people who have been sexually active in the past. But now they have also decided to be sexually abstinent until marriage.

If you are still a virgin and have decided to remain one until marriage, you are in an excellent position right now whether you realize it or not. You have not been exposed to the powerful sexual experience that, for some people, seems impossible to resist when single and unmarried. You haven't been emotionally or physically tied to anyone sexually, so your mind is able to keep its focus on God. You also haven't had to worry about pregnancy or sexually transmitted diseases.

It's a difficult struggle sometimes... It's like a "WAR"... A war with the flesh to abstain from sex for what sometimes seems like an eternity!

> But they that wait upon the Lord shall renew their strength; they shall mount up with wings as eagles; they shall run, and not be weary; and they shall walk, and not faint.
> *Isaiah 40:31*

If you have been sexually active in the past, you have made a great choice in committing to abstinence until marriage.

Sometimes, as you look back over your life, you may ask yourself, "Why did I choose to have sex before marriage?"

Was it because you thought that life as a virgin was archaic and decided to follow the advice of your peers? Was it

Presenting a Beautiful Body in the Eyes of God

because someone that claimed to love you and promised to marry you coerced you into sex, then disappeared in the night? The past is now gone. You can't go back and change it. But you can replace memories of the past with the never-ending memory of God. As you reach out to Him, He will renew a right spirit within you. It will be like starting your life all over again, as Jesus leads and guides you every step of the way ...

> I waited patiently for the Lord; and he inclined unto me, and heard my cry. He brought me up also out of an horrible pit, out of the miry clay, and set my feet upon a rock, and established my goings. And he hath put a new song in my mouth, even praise unto our God: many shall see it, and fear, and shall trust in the Lord.
> *Psalm 40:1-3*

There are some people in the world today that are on a hunt. They are searching for something more than the world has offered them so far. Some people may have chosen to imitate the standards of society and adopt them into their lives. Those standards have crippled the lives of many people. Satan has deposited false propaganda on the earth. That propaganda has covered our nation like a sheet, full of lies and deception.

How do we know that it's false? Listen to the Words of Jesus Himself. He said...

> Do not ye yet understand, that whatsoever entereth in at the mouth goeth into the belly, and is cast out into the draught? But those things which proceed out of the mouth come forth from the heart; and they defile the man. For out of the heart proceed evil thoughts, murders, adulteries,

fornications, thefts, false witness, blasphemies:
These are the things which defile a man…
Matthew 15:17-20a

The decision to remain abstinent until marriage can be one of the most demanding ones to make if you are not fully grounded with the Word of God. You may be utterly despised and misunderstood by those that have chosen to take a different journey. Some people will strike out at you verbally because of their sexual sins. They may refuse to ask God for forgiveness for those sins. Others have asked God for forgiveness. He has already forgiven them. But they won't forgive themselves. So they choose to insult you, instead. Others will mock you and laugh at you. You may be abandoned by someone close that claimed to love you- that is, until you decided to stop having sex with him/her. You may be labeled as weird, crazy or even homosexual. You may be treated by society as an outcast.

You may reach a point in your life where you begin to wonder if you really made the right decision after all. Is it worth the mistreatment that you may encounter from others that do not understand your decision?

You may face many lonely nights without a hand to hold, without an "I love you" to be emitted from the lips of a spouse. You may have a womb that seeks to be filled with a child. You may have loins that seek to father a child. You long to put on a beautiful wedding dress and walk down the aisle in front of hundreds of people. You constantly dream of the day when a father will give his daughter to you in marriage… You wonder if you will ever get your chance to fall in love and get married. It seems so easy to come by for those that choose to engage in premarital sex. The period of waiting seems endless at times.

Perhaps you have kept the faith and your mind fused to the Word of God, but now you can see the receding hairline,

Presenting a Beautiful Body in the Eyes of God

and the crow's feet emerge as you start to lose the battle with time. It seems as if your dreams are slowly fading away. You watch your biological clock start to decline, just like an hourglass. People that once kept the faith with you have either died or have stopped encouraging you. People that laughed at you years ago and said that you would never be married laugh louder because it appears that their predictions were accurate after all.

Do you have the faith to persevere... no matter what the outcome will be? Do you love the Lord so much that you will trust Him with that outcome?

I'm sure that if I had adopted worldly standards, I would have met a guy, had sex with him and possibly got married if I met his physical qualifications. I would not be single any longer and would finally have a husband and a family. But I would also have broken the heart of God in order to obtain it. That's not very much comfort to me when I realize that one day I will have to stand before the Lord and explain why I decided to choose the "easy way" out instead of trusting His Way.

Some people will get married when they are young—others will get married later in life, and some may never get married. Whatever the outcome, don't give up on God or lose faith in Him. If you give up on Him, you will lose so many blessings that await you...

> Has thou not known? Hast thou not heard, that the everlasting God, the Lord, the Creator of the ends of the earth, fainteth not, neither is weary? There is no searching of his understanding. He giveth power to the faint; and to them that have no might he increaseth strength.
>
> *Isaiah 40:28-29*

Illustration...

Jesus has a beautiful room ready just for me. It's full of every blessing, every dream that I have ever hoped to come true. I am coming to meet Him after traveling for many miles. He has been anticipating my arrival. He sees me coming up the road. I have my hands outstretched to Him and I am running to Him. He throws open the door and runs out to meet me. He smiles and says, "My lovely princess...You used to cry on my shoulder so many nights and I told you to just hold on a little longer, and now you've made it."

I then reach for the knob to the front door. But I suddenly stop and turn around because Satan is standing in the road with everything that I've been waiting on my whole life, also. I quickly grab it and run! Not caring where it came from, just as long as it's halfway close to what I asked for.

That's what you'll do if you attempt this journey, then turn and go back because it seems too long, lonely, and hard. You have just told God, "I love you, Man...but not that much...it takes too long to have. I don't have the rest of my life to wait...I want to have children. I'll be too old soon. I can't wait on You any longer."

Once you take this journey, don't look back. If you put temporary and fleshly desires before God, you have failed him already and won't be able to make such a sacrifice and be successful at it...

> And Jesus said unto him, No man, having put his hand to the plough, and looking back, is fit for the kingdom of God.
>
> *Luke 9:62*

2

The Revelation

∞

For as the rain cometh down, and the snow from heaven, and returneth not thither, but watereth the earth, and maketh it bring forth and bud, that it may give seed to the sower, and bread to the eater: So shall my word be that goeth forth out of my mouth; it shall not return unto me void , but it shall accomplish that which I please, and it shall prosper in the thing whereto I sent it.
Isaiah 55:10-11

Many people have asked me over the years how I was blessed to obtain knowledge about abstinence and why the gift of virginity is so important to me. I must confess that I didn't learn about it through the "normal channels". I didn't learn about it from my parents, from the church or from elderly women. I learned about abstinence when I began to study the Word of God.

I was saved when I was 13 years old. I was at a revival service at the church that I attended one night. Usually, I would fall asleep when I attended revival services, because

Stone the Builders Rejected

I really didn't understand everything the preacher talked about. On this occasion I listened to the preacher talk as I sat on the back pew of the church, folding a piece of paper into little squares. I listened to him talk about a man named Jesus Christ. He talked about His unending love for mankind. He said that He was my Friend and that He loved me. When he said the word "Friend," I immediately began to take more notice of the sermon.

During this period of time in my life, I was shy and without friends. I spent many years walking on the playground alone when I was in grade school. Kids picked on me in class on a daily basis. I was once hurled off a merry-go-round by a group of angry kids, and even had pencil shavings poured over my head when I was at my desk writing. I always seemed to be the person that was chosen last to play on a team. My classmates teased me because my clothes weren't the finest and because I was very quiet and meek. I was an easy target to attack because they knew that I wouldn't fight back. So when the preacher talked about Jesus, I knew that He was someone that I wanted to get to know. I wanted Him to be my friend because I didn't want to walk on the playground alone anymore. I wanted to have a friend that would remain with me forever. I wanted to make Jesus the Lord and Savior of my life.

So on this last night of revival services, the preacher gave an altar call for anyone that wanted to come up and accept Jesus as their Lord and Savior. I decided to go forward. But I was so shy and anxious that I was afraid to take that first step. I stood up nervously, and then slowly walked forward as my heart seemed to beat out of my chest.

It was as if I could just hear Him whisper to me, so softly...

"Come... Come here to me," Jesus smiled as He kneeled down and stretched out His Arms for me to come forward, to come closer to Him. So I did.

The Revelation

When I finally reached the altar, I felt Him standing next to me and I breathed a sigh of relief. I now had the opportunity to go to a beautiful place called Heaven. I finally had a Friend. This night I took the hand of Jesus and He accepted me just as I was.

Time passed and I eventually met a nice girl who remained a close earthly friend until we graduated from high school. But it was Jesus that I talked to at night. He was the one that I told all of my dreams to. It was Jesus who was captivated my heart and mind.

When I became a teenager, I found myself enchanted with the desire to have a boyfriend like the other girls in school. I would pray every night, hoping that the Lord would hear my prayer…yet nothing seemed to happen. I would often hear about sex in the girls' locker room at P.E. class in middle school. The girls fought to be as graphic as possible when talking about "it." They said that the loss of one's virginity was vital in order to become a "woman" and in order to keep a boyfriend.

"Well, that doesn't make sense," I would whisper to myself, "Why would anyone want to go through all of that just to get somebody's jacket or class ring?"

I sat on the sofa at home one evening, thumbing through the Bible. I searched for a passage that permitted sex before marriage; I wasn't able to find one. I did, however find a verse that spoke to the contrary…

> Flee fornication. Every sin that a man doeth is without the body; but he that committeth fornication sinneth against his own body.
> *I Corinthians 6:18*

If this is the will of God, why would people would choose to do the opposite just for the sake of having a moment of pleasure? Perhaps there were bigger problems in the world than fornication. Perhaps people participated in fornication because they, like myself, had never been told about abstinence. Whatever the reason was, I didn't know. I just knew in my spirit, that if it was something that wasn't pleasing to God, it wasn't pleasing to me, either.

As I began to read the Bible more, I had a desire to spend more time with God. Some people are afraid to get close to Him, maybe because they're afraid that they'll have to give up a lukewarm Christian life. I've learned that when I've allowed God to come closer to me, my life is comforted. He's so Wonderful...

Spending time with God involves more than a weekly Sunday message at church. It should be a lifetime process that never grows old. As I've gotten older, I've come to understand that it's God that gives me life. No one has the ability to breathe life into the nostrils of a human being, or to form snow-capped mountains and vibrant waterfalls. I find myself constantly in awe of His Opulent Wisdom and Timeless Knowledge. He is Perfect, Holy, and Sovereign... These are signs that temporal man chooses to ignore. Man cannot stop a hurricane, tornado or flood...yet he creates his own laws and shakes a fist at God when those laws cause his own destruction. Every law that God has created to help man, carnal mankind has taken and destroyed because of its refusal to be submissive to Him... The evolution of murder, adultery, abortion, rape, fornication, immorality, war, alcoholism and drugs evolved because of the sin of Adam and Eve. Now that sin has sifted its way into the heart of our nation in order to annihilate every generation that we give birth to.

It was always God's Will that sex be reserved for marriage. Now the promotion of a sex-saturated society has hardened the heart of the masses. Satan now encourages society to fashion sex into an idol to worship. He wants it to be worshipped so that we can worship his evil presence instead of God. It is forced to become something lewd and is made as graphic as possible. It must be degrading. It must mortify the beauty of the human body and the heart. The beauty of sex has been snatched away by the lechery of lustful individuals and modified to satisfy the flesh. It is the flesh that becomes furious and rebels against being controlled and brought under submission. As a result, sex after marriage is overruled and sexual promiscuity becomes the norm.

An individual that is truly searching to please God will not attempt to manipulate anything that He has created for our good. God is sovereign over the heaven and the earth- Not us. Guess what else? He's smarter than us. He'll always be right- We'll always be wrong unless what we say is what He says.

I decided to follow Jesus and to be obedient to Him, no questions asked.Why? Because I could have ended up as a teenage mother,abandoned and alone, or with a sexually transmitted disease. I could have ended up like that because no one had ever told me about the precious gift of virginity and God's Will for me to remain one until marriage. I found myself becoming angry at times when I thought about things that could have happened to me. But for some reason, God chose to whisper that message into my ear. From that moment on, I made a declaration to Him that I would not rest until every person that I came into contact with knew the message of abstinence as well. There's something about abstinence that boggles the average human mind.But the aroma of its blessing is sweet in the nostrils of Jesus.I will never forget what God did for me in that instant that no one else even considered doing. Because of that very special blessing, I decided to become His servant and follow Him wherever He would lead me. He knew that through me His Word would not return void.

3

Because of the Love of the Father

∞

> Children obey your parents in all things: for this is well pleasing unto the Lord.
> *Colossians 3:20*

It's such a wonderful blessing to have parents that love and care for you like my parents do! As I have matured in age, I sometimes think back over my life, and remember so many sacrifices that they made for me. They wanted to shield and protect me from anything that could cause me harm. They wanted me to have the very best that they had to offer.

When I was 5 years old, I was afflicted with a case of bronchitis. I remember being afraid to go to sleep because I feared that I'd never wake up again. My breathing was so labored that I couldn't turn any particular way and have peace resting.

But eventually I would drift off to sleep. My eyes would open and close sometimes when I would feel a blanket being pulled up over my shoulders by my parents as they sat by my bed, staring at with me with concern.

All through the night, I would wake up periodically and watch them take turns pacing back and forth, waiting for the medication to hurry up and take effect so I could feel better.

The concern of my parents over my safety reminded me of the concern that the Lord had over my life as well. They wanted the best for my life, and He did too.

I haven't been blessed with the opportunity to be a parent yet. But I certainly understand the tremendous responsibility of parenting. I can sympathize with a parent whose child has died. It is like having someone rip a part of your body out of its foundation, and no matter how many years come and go, you will never forget that child, because that baby was a part of you. That's how the Lord feels when we allow Satan to lure us away from Him. It's like we have been separated from His Warm, Loving Bosom… He's searching for us… He calls out for us to come back home… He loves us so much… He even gave up His Only Son and offered Him as a sacrifice so that we could always have the opportunity to come back home…

One of my good friends, Michelle Gowan expressed her love for her daughter Lauren…

> "…My daughter, Lauren Elizabeth Gowan, born Valentine's Day, 2000, is truly a gift from God… She has a smile and a little giggle that will melt your heart…She is such a wonderful blessing to me…I will always treasure my little sweetheart…"

I've also noticed through the relationship that I have with my nieces and nephews that I want to protect them from any hurt or pain that they may face. As they grow up, I still see them as helpless babies and it's really tough to watch them become young adults. I finally see through the eyes of my parents how hard it must have been for them to see me grow up.

God feels the same way about us. We get upset sometimes when we want something and we don't get it when we want it. Sometimes we may never get it. The whole point is that God knows what we need. He also knows what we don't need. That's the reason why He gave us laws to go by in the Word of God...He doesn't want to see us hurt because we're His babies... He wants us to have the very best in our lives.

Living a life of holiness shows a respect and reverence for Our Father. This is the reason why some people have lives that are full of chaos and turmoil. They answer only to themselves. We worship God by to having respect for our bodies. After all, the body is the temple of God. God dwells inside of us. We care for our bodies when we refuse to put anything in it that God wouldn't approve of.. If there's anything that's put into the body that alters it in a negative way, it doesn't belong there. Smoking, drugs, and alcohol shouldn't be a part of God's temple. Eating food that's unhealthy is bad for God's temple. Sexual promiscuity has no place in God's temple. It is through these channels that many problems begin.

We respect God's temple in the way we speak, also. Nothing is more repugnant to the ears than having to listen to a person that walks around with a mouth full of filthy words. Sometimes, when I have been talking to a group of people, I would hear someone curse, then say something like, "Excuse me, I'm sorry." They were more concerned about offending me than offending God, the one that created them. Some people believe that cursing, lying, and using profane language makes them cute and popular. It doesn't help them. It hurts them. God does not condone profanity that is inside or outside of His temple.

We respect God and His temple by having a positive outlook on life and not by listening to people that are always pessimistic about life. They focus on the world's events and remain glued to the television and newspaper trying to find hope through people.

That's such a tragedy, because the temple of God, which is our bodies, becomes a beautiful thing to behold when it's removed of all of the things that don't belong there. The only hope that our temples should hold is hope in God.

> What? Know ye not that your body is the temple of the Holy Ghost which is in you, which ye have of God and ye are not your own? For ye are bought with a price: therefore glorify God in your body, and in your spirit, which are God's.
> *I Corinthians 7:19-20*

The choice to remain abstinent until marriage is important to me because I don't want to grieve the heart of God by giving a part of myself away—A part that He has ordained to be a precious gift to give only to my husband.... Not a friend, acquaintance, boyfriend or one-night stand. I have learned that the goal is not to please myself temporarily with a man that I can see and touch but to please God, The One that I can't see and touch but love even greater than flesh and bone...

4

Following the Master

∞

...And as Jesus passed forth from thence, he saw a man, named Matthew, sitting at the receipt of custom: and he saith unto him, Follow me...And he arose, and followed him.

Matthew 9:9

I went to college when I was 18 years old. I was so excited about college because I was finally going to get the opportunity to pursue my goal of becoming a physician. I also knew in my heart that I would finally get my first boyfriend, fall in love, graduate, and get married. That was my plan.

I didn't hide the fact from anyone that I was a Christian. I was also a Christian that refused to back down from my standards. My peers learned quickly that if I had to make a choice between their words and the Words of God, they would lose. I had made a decision to put God first in everything that I did. In order to be able to follow Jesus for life, you must get out of the crutch of worrying about what others think. Some peers will laugh at you and call you names when you take a stand for Christ. If you worry about what a person thinks about you, you haven't really committed to Him.

I majored in Biology. I had a great desire to become a pediatrician. I thought about it all of the time. I loved reading about the human body and how it worked, especially the heart. By the time I entered high school, I was sure that I wanted to be physician.

As I entered my second year of college, however, I found myself spending more time listening to people's problems than concentrating on Biology classes. They always seemed to think that I had an answer to their boyfriend conflicts (although I'd never had a boyfriend). They thought I had all the answers to their emotional and spiritual problems. (Although there were many brothers and sisters in Christ that were also willing to lend an ear.)

One night as I slept soundly, I had a beautiful dream. It would be one that I would remember for the rest of my life.

In the dream, the Lord had His Arm around my waist and He was carrying me past branches and vines as we soared in the air. The thing that I remember the most about Him was feeling completely safe because He was close to me...

He finally released me and placed me on the ground. There was light all around me and I looked down to see where I was. I could remember Him say only two words as His Hands stretched out to me...

"Follow me..."

As I looked up to see who it was that was telling me to follow Him, I woke up. I stared around my dorm room. I only saw my roommate snoring, sound asleep.

I never really thought about the dream any more. After a period of time, I then began to face one misfortune after another. I encountered money problems, car problems, and illness. I was unable to concentrate on my studies. I couldn't understand why so many bad things were happening in my life even though I was living my life for the Lord. I knew that being saved didn't give me a ticket to live an easy and carefree life, a life without worries. But I wanted God to help me find an answer to these problems. I wondered what it was that I was doing wrong that hindered me from my dream of being a physician.

I prayed to the Lord about my situation. He revealed to me that He had another plan for my life. Unfortunately, it wasn't a career in medicine. I was brokenhearted. I cried, pleaded and begged for Him to change His mind. When He refused to do that, I rebelled against Him and enrolled for a fourth year in college. Even though I had attempted to begin, my conscience would not allow me to continue. I couldn't understand why God wouldn't let me have my heart's desire. And what was His plan? What did He have that was better than what I wanted?

I discovered through my experience of trying to go in a different direction than God had ordained for me that I had two choices... Surrender to His Will for my life, or to continue to obtain a degree that He had refused for my future and destroy myself trying.

That's why it's so important to always ask God for His Will when you are trying to make a decision about something. If His Will is your will, then it's foolproof and can't go wrong unless you cause it to go wrong. Many people will obtain a job just for the money and loathe the position. Some people go from job to job, seeking to find one that will give them satisfaction and struggle finding it. I believe that you should choose a job that you would want to do more than anything in the world. You should choose a job that you would do, even if you weren't paid to do it.

I made a selfish decision to continue to work towards my

college degree. Why? It was because I was too ashamed to face my family and friends. I thought of myself as a failure for not completing my degree...It was only a grasp away...

Suddenly all of the plans that I'd made were gone. I didn't get the boyfriend and I didn't get the opportunity to become a physician.

Now I made a decision to follow the words of a loving God that couldn't be wrong. So I packed up that fall quarter after 3 years of college and went back home. What was God's plan? I had no idea.

5

Listening to His Voice

∞

> Come unto me, all ye that labour and are heavy laden and I will give you rest. Take my yoke upon you, and learn of me; for I am meek and lowly in heart and you shall find rest unto your souls…For my yoke is easy and my burden is light.
> *Matt. 11:28*

I left college and moved back in with my parents. During that period of time I had a series of jobs. They included factory and hospital work. Sometimes I would think back and wonder what my life would be like now if I had become a doctor. I could have spent my life helping sick people get well. I couldn't understand God's plan. I definitely didn't see it in the jobs that I had obtained over the years. None of them were fulfilling. As I would later discover, He would use each job experience to help me accomplish the plan that He had for my life.

As I rested on the sofa at home one evening, I reflected back over the years that I had spent in college listening to my peers as they discussed their problems. Over that period of time I had encountered many men and women that had lowered their standards sexually in order to find "true love."

One of my good friends in particular, was in love with a guy that didn't love her. Because she harbored low self-esteem, she compromised her values and provided him with a sexual relationship and all of the money his heart desired.

Another guy thought that by having sex with a lot of women, he would be popular. He believed that he could be "saved" and still be sexually active without being married. Another guy said that I had to be insane to shut myself off from the pleasurable gift of sex that was out there to enjoy freely without any strings or emotions attached.

Sometimes people won't choose a godly mate. They won't choose someone that has good character and integrity. I once knew a young lady that was desperate to continue a relationship with her boyfriend. When she told him that she was pregnant, he ordered her to have an abortion if she wanted to remain with him. She came to me for advice. I told her that any guy who would order her to have an abortion cared nothing about her but everything about himself. Having an abortion would help her gain nothing but an emotional torment that no human could fix.

She went out of town and had the abortion anyway. The next day the guy had moved out and never called her again. She ended up without a boyfriend and a baby. She decided to listen to "words" from a spiritually illiterate human being instead of the Word of God.

Some people have been emotionally scarred, sometimes as a result of divorce (their parents), or by violence and abuse during their childhood that hasn't been resolved through prayer and healing. They carry those wounds inside of them. They spend nights alone in tears, reaching out for a love that seems so far away. Their self-esteem has been shattered and sleep refuses to give them any rest. The heart that was once a beautiful rose has become bruised and battered. They no longer care about being hurt, just as long as they have somebody…anybody at all.

They feel that the only way to obtain love is through sex.

They feel that sexual relationships will make their emptiness go away. They think that sexual relationships will make them feel loved. Sexual relationships never make you feel loved. They are just relationships that steal your self—respect away and lower your self-esteem. They are relationships that separate you from God.

They are trying to put a human being before God. They search for the perfect person that will take away all of their misery and pain and make them complete. The truth is, only God can complete you and make you a whole person.

This topic is especially important which it comes to abstinence. You can live your life for the Lord and choose to be abstinent until marriage. But you can still end up with an advocate of Satan if you allow low-self esteem or fear of being alone to hinder you from what God has to give you. That's why we must allow God to bring our mates to us. We must trust Him with that decision and not try to "help Him out."

For example, Satan can send a man along that will tell a woman everything that she's always wanted to hear. He'll say anything in order to get what he wants. If he's searching for sex, he'll pursue her and tell her that she's the most beautiful woman in the world. He'll meticulously fool her into believing that sex is the ultimate sacrifice to make in order to have a lifetime of love with him.

He might start out by making a lot of promises to her. He knows that she desires more from a relationship than sex. So he'll promise to marry her if she'll have sex with him. She may tell herself that she won't lower her standards and fall in such a trap. But slowly she starts to accept things that she once wouldn't accept. He will refuse any Biblical principle about abstinence as some old tale that was outdated thousands of years ago. Every thing that lines up with the word of God, he will refute. And just suppose she ends up pregnant or with a sexually transmitted disease?

Suddenly "love grows thin." He eventually fades off in the sunset. If she ends up pregnant, she is suddenly alone with no one to help her raise the baby. She may end up discovering that she has AIDS. What happened to the invincible love and the marriage and all of the promises then? When young women make the decision to have sex with as many men as it takes in order to obtain a wedding ring, they seem to lose themselves in the process. Their hearts become hard. They look tired, sad, and angry. They look this way because a worldly process has failed them. Even if they make it through the maze and get married, some of them may wonder what life would have been like if they had just done it God's way.

There have been instances where young men have been seduced by the words of women as well. In today's culture, there are some young women that are allowing themselves to get pregnant, hoping that they can hold on to their boyfriends. They had hoped to get married by having sex with the guy and it didn't work. So they hope that, by becoming pregnant, the guy will stay. Sometimes the guy doesn't even really love the young lady. He may just be interested in a sexual relationship. If the young lady gets pregnant, he may still break up with her. This leaves a trail of child support payments and babies that may never see their fathers on a daily basis. They may wonder what life would have been like if they had just waited until marriage to have sex. Those little acts of sexual pleasure end up costing us greatly in the end. It's Satan's mission to enter our lives and destroy the plans that God has made for us. He will whisper sweet words in our ears, telling us that everything will work out just fine. Then he walks away when we're in trouble and it seems like there's no way out. We do it God's way by entrusting our fleshly desires to Him. We spend our

Listening to His Voice

time focused on Him. Instead of trying to pressure someone into doing something that's against the Will of God, we treasure that person's decision. We value them as a precious jewel that loves God more than anything in the world. We wouldn't do anything to break their heart, because we know that if we break their heart, we also break the heart of God. Don't pressure young women to have sex with you, young men. If they chose to remain abstinent until marriage and you didn't, move on. Don't waste time making them promises that you know you won't keep. Don't allow your body to be terrorized by having sex with men in order to find love, young women. If it takes all of that to find it, you never needed it to begin with.

True, the sexual desire is always there. It's way we were created. People that choose to be abstinent refuse to act on those desires. It's not because they're scared that God will send fire from heaven and consume them. Waiting until marriage to have sex lines up with what the Lord expects. To remain a virgin until marriage is not as unusual as some people tend to think.

Critics label us as unrealistic creatures. We are not unrealistic. We are creatures grafted from the Vine of Jesus Christ and have made a choice to place those desires in His Hands and not our own. If we keep them in our own hands, we will fail. If we give them to Him, we will win…

6

Hope Grows Dim

∞

> Judge me, O Lord; for I have walked in mine integrity: I have trusted also in the Lord; therefore I shall not slide. Examine me, O Lord, and prove me; try my reins and my heart. For thy lovingkindness is before mine eyes: and I have walked in thy truth.
>
> *Psalm 26:1-3*

I had a devised a plan when I began college. I was going to become a doctor. I was going to finally get the boyfriend that I had always wanted, get married after school, and live happily ever after. But that plan didn't work out just the way that I wanted it to. So I devised another plan. I would meet a nice guy on my job, fall in love with him, and get married. I would get married at 26, have a baby at 28 and live happily ever after. I would have a beautiful home with a white picket fence surrounding it. I would have a beautiful lawn and a pool in the back yard. I would spend the evenings out on my patio with my wonderful husband. I'd be sipping lemonade and wearing my cool shades, as I watched my kids play happily in their sand box. I just knew that this plan was a good one and it would definitely work. After all, I had followed the Lord and was obedient to Him. I had always tried to do the right thing. I did everything that He told me to do, even when it didn't seem to make sense, sometimes. So I believed that I would be blessed to receive everything my heart desired according to my new plan.

It didn't happen. I didn't meet anyone on my job, or anywhere else for that matter. I prayed every night for my dream to come true. I counted every year, praying and waiting for my plan to quickly evolve. I began to worry when I turned 25. I began to cry when I turned 26. I made a new plan at 28. This time I would pray to get married at 28 and have a baby at 30. It didn't happen. I began to pray frantically for my plan to be enforced. I began to ask God what was wrong with me. Why couldn't I meet a nice guy and fall in love with him? I couldn't understand.

I was now living in my own apartment. Sometimes, I would get so lonely. I HATED being single. I would sit in my room on every birthday and holiday and get depressed. I would see my siblings get nice presents for Christmas and Valentine's Day and I would get nothing. I began to dread special occasions because I was the only one that never had anyone special to share my holidays with.

Every time someone would come up to me and tell me that they were engaged, my heart would break. I couldn't understand why it was so hard for me to meet someone and so easy for everyone else.

Another friend attempted to "help me out." She was going to introduce me to one of her husband's friends.

"He's a real nice guy and all," she began, as we chatted on the phone.

"I'm sure he is," I responded.

"I'm going to tell my husband that you'd be interested then," she added, "But you know, you have to have sex with him if you want him for a boyfriend or he's not going to stay.

That's just the way it is today."

"I thought you said that he was a nice guy…"

"He is," she laughed, " But sex is a very important issue for guys. Are you still interested? Do you want me to tell my husband when he gets off work?"

"No," I sighed, "I'm not interested. You know where I stand on that."

"Okay, suit yourself, then. You're going to be alone forever. There aren't any guys out there that are going to take you out if you don't have sex with them sooner or later. That's why nobody ever asks you out."

"I've heard. Thanks anyway," I sighed, as I hung up the phone.

I continued to create my plan for marriage and children until I became 30. After that, I began to lose hope of ever finding anyone to share my life with. I had nothing to show for all of my years of being faithful to God. I had done everything the right way and I was still single and alone. I didn't see God's plan. I didn't see anything. I began to feel sorry for myself. I felt as if I was stuck in an impossible maze. I knew that sex before marriage was wrong. But it seemed that the only way to meet someone and get married was to submit to premarital sex.

It wasn't an option for me.

I can't count all of the times that I would pray for God to bless me with a mate. Each holiday would come and go. Every birthday flew by like a hurricane. I would find myself in tears as I slowly watched all of my siblings meet and fall in love with the right person. And there was nobody for me.

Some of my Christian friends would say, "It's just not your time, yet. Just wait on God. He'll send you someone really great." But honestly in my heart, I had heard that so many times and for so many years, that I was tired of hearing it.

I would read my Bible and try to concentrate on the verses that dealt with faith. But I would still wake up in the morning, worried about remaining single for the rest of my life.

"What's wrong with me, Lord? What have I done so wrong that no one will marry me?" I cried out one night, as I sat up in my bed, sobbing.

"Why won't you trust me?" He asked.

"I do trust you, Lord...I trust you with my whole life. I've given my whole life to you," I answered, as I looked up at Him with swollen eyes.

"You don't trust me enough, love. You haven't given your whole life to me," He spoke gently.

"I tried to do the right thing and look at me! The only people that get what they want are the ones that do what they want to! I bet if I was like everybody else and acted like everybody else I'd be married in a heartbeat!" I retorted.

"Do you want to be like everyone else?" He asked.

"No, I don't..."

"Then why won't you trust me?"

"I do trust you, Lord... But why is everybody getting blessed but me?" I asked.

"Don't trust you? I don't understand," I whispered to myself, as I fell back against my pillow.

He was right. I didn't trust Him with my whole life.

But as I slowly drifted off to sleep, Jesus sat on my bed and watched over me all night long. He really wanted me to be happy and to trust Him. But it wasn't something that He would do for me.

7

The Final Shattered Plan

∞

> ...A good man out of the treasure of his heart bring forth that which is good; and an evil man out of the evil treasure of his heart bringeth forth that which is evil; for of the abundance of the heart his mouth speaketh.
>
> *Luke 6:45*

I was now 35 years old. I was still in an endless search to discover the great plan that God had for my life... I had abandoned my desires to meet His, yet it seemed as if there wasn't a plan for my life. I had fought to push the desire to be married behind me. But occasionally I would have waves of loneliness that would float back and forth in my mind. I had obtained a new job at a hospital. It was a good job, but now it had become harder to attend church because I had to work on Sundays. The majority of people that I worked with didn't support abstinence. They would constantly tell me that I would never meet or marry any guy if I didn't have sex with him first. Sex was the golden seal to the relationship and without it there was no relationship. I knew in my heart that their philosophy was out of the question. I started to become anxious about my life as a single person. I started to believe that my dream of getting married and having a great career wasn't possible, based on the words of worldly people. All of the faith that I thought I had in my possession slowly began to unravel all around me.

I forced myself to read the Word of God, praying that my fear of the unknown would be put behind me. I was struggling to believe that God had a good plan waiting for me if I would just trust Him with the outcome. But I couldn't see the outcome.

I went on blind dates. Each one left me disillusioned about ever falling in love and getting married one day. My friends saw these guys as okay. So they smoked, or maybe drank a little. But at least they didn't physically abuse me. I looked at the situation differently. I was looking for someone that loved God more than anything, even me. If they had to make the choice between God and me, they would choose God. I was looking for that because I felt those same way about Him. That was the piece of puzzle that I was searching for. I longed to have someone that I could go to church with. I longed to have someone that I could pray with. I wanted someone that I could hold hands with and tell all of my dreams to... But "I" wasn't able to find that person.

I was sitting across the dinner table, asking this guy about his likes and dislikes. Yes, he had a Master's degree in two subjects and had a good job. But he wasn't saved, nor did he attend church regularly. He wasn't what I was looking for.

I had a second blind date with a guy that had been saved for a few years. He was someone that had a nice personality and a good sense of humor. I decided not to go out on another date with him again, however. He called me one evening- He wanted to know when we were going to "get together."

"Most people your age have already had sex by now," he quipped.

The Final Shattered Plan

"That's what I've heard," I said as I stared blankly into the television screen.

"I mean, I think you're a nice girl and all, but that's just part of having a relationship. We're kind of at a standstill."

"Didn't I tell you that I didn't believe in sex before marriage?" I snapped.

"Yea, you said that but I thought you were kidding," he laughed, "I mean, get real... 35?"

Then there was silence.

"Did you hear me?" he asked.

"Yep."

Silence.

"I mean, there are a lot of girls that want to ask me out and all, and I've still waited for you," he stated bluntly.

Silence.

"Did you hear me?"

"I sure did," I replied.

"Does any of it make sense?"

"Oh, all of it makes perfect sense to me," I said, as I started to flip through the channels.

"Good," he said with a big sigh of relief, "So when are we going to get together?"

"Oh I can tell you that right now," I answered, "Close your eyes".

"Okay, they're closed."

"What do you see?"

"Nothing yet..."

"Wow, neither do I," I replied.

"What does that mean? I don't get it."

Click.

The process continued, and "I" had frankly grown tired of hitting dead ends. I was now certain that I would just shrivel up and die an old maid with no great destiny and no Prince Charming.

People had started to criticize me and say that I was too

Stone the Builders Rejected

---

difficult and too picky because of my standards.

As Christians we must understand that Satan despises us. He will do anything in his power to keep us apart from God. How does he accomplish this? He is the master manipulator. He knows how to find our weak places and use them against us if we are not grounded in the Word of God. In order to fight off the devil we must allow God to take charge of our lives totally. I had trusted Him in every area of my life. But I didn't trust Him as far as "my plans" for marriage were concerned. I was afraid that if I gave this part of my life to Him I would end up as a 100-year-old woman who finally found the right guy but was too old to spend very many years with him.

Satan knew that one of the greatest desires of my life was to be married. I had never had a boyfriend before and had never had anyone around long enough to develop any type of relationship with. I was so full of love and had so much love to give someone. I was just bursting inside to tell someone about the Lord and how He good He had been to me. I longed to have someone that I could love and someone that could love me back.

Gradually, I started to feel that I had missed out on what God had planned for my life.

My faith continued to waver just like the waves of a sea. One day I would be optimistic about my future. The next minute I would be frantic, wondering what my future would hold. I believed that if "I" could just get a boyfriend, fall in love with him and get married, then God would tell me what His plan was for my life. Then I would live happily ever after.

Illustration...

Satan sat in his chambers in Hades staring at his sect of young men. He knew about the great plan that God had for my life long before I was to find out. He had to stop it from happening...

The Final Shattered Plan

The man stood before him and stared directly at him, waiting for instructions.

"There is a woman on the earth...I despise her and I suppose that's no secret to anyone here...I hate her very life...I hate her relationship with this Jesus who is also called Christ...Her devotion to Him is disgusting! ... She is being jettisoned to assist with the destruction of this kingdom and I want her stopped by any means necessary...I don't care how you do it," he growled.

The man left the room and searched for me. He made it his mission to succeed where others had failed. He found a body to place his demonic presence into, someone that lived a life separate from God. He stepped into this body and began his mission.

I met this guy at work. He seemed to be someone that really loved God. He also knew a lot about the Bible. He showered me with jewelry, clothes, and phone calls. He didn't carry any emotional baggage. He didn't even have children! He had a tender heart and a sweet spirit and was very humorous. What I liked best about this guy was that he supported me with my stand on abstinence. I had started to believe that perhaps this was the person that "I" had been searching for all of my life. We discussed traveling to far away places and even getting married in the future. It seemed too good to be true, and of course it was.

He never went to church with me. He began to change his opinion on sex. He told me that our relationship had the potential to grow, but only if we had sex first. I was devastated. I couldn't believe that it was happening to me again. I really felt that "I" had finally found the right guy and now he was giving me an ultimatum. If I didn't agree to his terms, he would go and find someone else who would.

He stopped calling me. I didn't get a single phone call for a whole week. My friends could tell that I wasn't as happy as I had been when I first met my "Knight in Shining

Stone the Builders Rejected

Armor." When I told them about my dilemma, one of my co-workers pulled me aside and gave me some advice.

"Listen," she began, "He seems to be a real nice guy. He doesn't have any kids, either. That's hard to find these days."

Then she began to whisper.

"Listen, if I were you, I'd sleep with him just one time. I really believe he would stay with you then. Then ask God to forgive you. Why don't you try that? If you don't, he's going to be gone, girl."

A close Christian friend talked to me on the phone as she was preparing dinner for her family.

"I wouldn't talk to that jerk ever again. You're better off without him. God will bless you with somebody good. Just don't give up."

He called me back after two weeks.

"Well, have you thought about what we discussed before?" he asked. In a matter of seconds, I could see my whole life flash before my eyes. I was now 36 years old. I had absolutely no prospects for marriage. I had no destiny. I had nothing. "I" had been searching for true love all of my life. "I" was unable to find it. I had grown so tired of hearing guys say that I wasn't good enough for them unless I had something to offer them first.

I could hear myself telling God "I'm so tired of this...I'm so tired, God..."

I had a decision to make. I could choose to have sex with him and have an instant boyfriend. It was what I had been waiting for my whole life. I'd have a good chance of getting married. He did mention that at one time. I would have children and a happy home. I could stay at my job and work towards the destiny that God had for my life. Maybe God's plan was at the hospital where I worked now.

I could see Satan standing on one side of the room with his arms folded, trying to torment me.

"This is your last chance...You'd better grab it while you

The Final Shattered Plan

can! You may never find any body else like this again...He asked you out on more than one date...Get a load of that! Go for it! You'll regret it if you don't..."

Then I could see Jesus standing at the door, smiling at me. He never said a word, never gave me any advice... He just stood there and smiled at me for what seemed like an eternity. Then He blew me a kiss, turned, and left.

"Well, what did you decide?" the guy asked.

"I can't do that," I uttered.

"Well, if you don't, something bad is going to happen," he voiced angrily.

He never called again.

8

Pain Exposed in the Presence of a Loving God

∞

> Whomsoever cometh to me, and heareth my sayings, and doeth them, I will shew you to whom he is like: He is like a man which built an house, and digged deep, and laid the foundation on a rock; and when the flood arose, the stream beat vehemently upon that house, and could not shake it: for it was founded upon a rock. But he that heareth and doeth not, is like a man that without a foundation built a house upon the earth; against which the stream did beat vehemently, and immediately it fell; And the ruin of the house was great.
>
> *Luke 6:46-49*

As the months raged on in my life I became even more anxious about my destiny. "I" had failed miserably to discover the great plan of God. "I" had failed to find my Knight in Shining Armor as well. I felt that my whole life

Stone the Builders Rejected

was one big failure. The humiliation of repeated rejections by guys had taken its toll on me. I had become calloused and hard in my heart.

I stared blankly into space and tried to make sense of my life. I knew that there was something that I was capable of doing, but I still didn't know what it was. Why couldn't "I" find the destiny that troubled my heart so miserably that I couldn't find peace? Why couldn't "I" find that one true love of my life so I could finally be happy?

I remember the words of a Christian friend that tried to encourage me...

"You weren't meant to be someone's floor mat...You were meant to be someone's wife...That's why those people never stayed with you...They weren't able to see beyond their flesh...They weren't willing to make an investment in you. You deserve better than that..." he assured me.

He and his fiancée had everything that I'd been searching for. They were both still virgins and were getting married in two weeks. They had finally found true love with each other. If it could work for them, why couldn't it work for me?

I had spent many years listening to my unsaved friends tell me that it was virtually impossible to find anyone that would wait until marriage for sex. Everything in the world seemed to say that sexual promiscuity was the wave of the future. I felt as if I was the only person on earth that cared about doing what was right. I felt like I was standing up for what was right and getting punished for it. I was getting laughed at, mocked and called names for daring to be different.

I was so scared to trust God. I was afraid that I would never get married or have children. I was afraid that I would never discover this magnificent plan that God had promised me. It had consumed every day of my life. I felt that I had been cheated out of the great happiness that everyone else had and I was helpless to do anything about it.

Pain Exposed in the Presence of a Loving God

Satan laughed, "You're nothing but a hypocrite...You tell everybody else what a normal relationship looks like and you can't even keep one single man...You talk about how much He loves you ...If He loves you so much, then why are you still by yourself? You need to face reality, chick! Who do you think is going to want somebody like you? Getting married, yea right! Nobody wants a woman that doesn't have any sexual experience...Children...You're too old! It's all over for you and you know it! You're all washed up Just give up...You're a has-been. He's forgotten all about you. Plan...There IS no plan...Why don't you just quit! You don't know what faith is...You don't have any faith...Just look at yourself... You're a loser...You're a failure...You're nothing..."

I chose to ignore him. But inside I did feel like a failure. I felt like I was incomplete as a woman because I couldn't find a husband and because I was childless. I was working at a job that I didn't like and wishing that something else would come my way. I wanted a job that I enjoyed doing more than anything else in the world.

I didn't feel like sitting at home alone that evening, so decided to go to my parents' house and spend the night.

They sat with me and watched television. No one said a word. They had heard all of the stories and saw the sadness in my face over each dating failure until it had started to play like a broken record in their ears. I felt the tension in the room as one of them wanted to say something, but didn't know what to say.

They had watched me over the years visit them with a beaming smile, so excited to tell them that I had met a new guy, only to visit days or weeks later to announce to them that he was no longer interested. But tonight, we sat and watched a gospel music video. Eventually, they went to bed and I was left alone.

The video continued to play. The singer talked about all

of the pain that he had endured in his life. He talked about God and how He had brought him through each obstacle. The songs ministered to my heart. Each song he performed seemed as if it were meant for me to hear.

As the evening went on and the music video continued to play, I felt my heart began to ache. My stomach became weak and nausea began to consume me. I felt it being stepped on, twisted and tied into knots. Someone else was trying to get close to my heart. But I refused to allow anyone to break it again.

I wouldn't allow anyone to know what I was feeling inside... I would hide the pain within me and no one would know...

I could hear myself saying, "You can't have it...I won't let you have my heart...You can't have it...I don't have to have anybody in my life...I don't need anybody...I can make it by myself...I'm so tired of being sad...I'm so tired of being alone...So tired...Lord, I'm so tired... "

As I sat on the sofa the words pounded in my ears like a freight train. But I refused to believe that I should pray for the desire of my heart one more time. Perhaps it just wasn't God's Will for me to have a family of my own. As I sat there with my head dropped and my eyes staring at the carpet, I could hear these words... "Why art thou cast down, O my soul? And why art thou disquieted in me? Hope thou in God: for I shall yet praise him for the help of his countenance... As I looked up towards heaven I could hear Jesus say... "Give your heart to me ...Will you trust me now?"

I could see a beautiful chiseled hand reaching out to take the trembling ones that lay folded in my lap. I sank weakly to my knees, gripping my hands around a folding chair as tightly as I could.

As the video played, the music became soundless as I stared at the seat of that chair. I wanted to say something to Jesus, but nothing would come from my lips. I couldn't get

Pain Exposed in the Presence of a Loving God

my mouth to move or to utter a word. I wanted to tell Him how sorry I was that "I" had tried to find my own husband and my own destiny. I wanted to tell Him how sorry I was for allowing people to come and go in my life that He had never put there in the first place. I knew that He didn't want me to be unevenly yoked to a guy that was unsaved. Yet I went out on dates with some guys that were unsaved. I wanted to tell Him how sorry I was that I had allowed the desire to get married to dominate His Will for my life. I wanted to tell Him that it was my fault that my destiny hadn't surfaced. I wanted His Forgiveness for sinning against Him with my selfishness and with my pride. I wanted Him to give me a second chance because I had allowed the ways of the world to bring me down so low. I had failed Him miserably and I couldn't forgive myself.

I had to make a decision. My Lord was answering my prayer. He was asking me to trust Him and to give my heart to Him, broken, bleeding, and wounded. He wanted me to give my whole life over to Him and to trust the outcome and I was afraid to. The champion for Christ, the unbreakable rock, the one that was sealed to the faith was now afraid to let go of my whole life and give it to the One that created it.

I was unable to express what I felt in my heart. I stared at the seat of the chair, full of humiliation and grief...

I begin to weep silently as my parents slept in the other room. Jesus knelt next to me, draped His Arm around my shoulder and held me gently. My life began to pass before my eyes and I began to see all of the broken and cracked places before me that I refused to mourn over. I began to see all of the days that my womb wept for a baby to fill it but was barren and void instead. I began to see all of the dreams that I had wanted to come true, but had now become an empty void. I began to see all of the broken promises from uncaring guys and wedding dresses that had never been worn, but were instead dresses, empty and void.

I wanted to be the happy person that I used to be before my innocent heart was hardened by things that I should have never allowed to enter it. I wanted to be me again.

I cried out for Him to tell me what was wrong with me, why I never seemed to fit anywhere, why I was so out of place, why no one wanted me, why nobody cared about me or loved me. I trembled as I screamed within myself as Hannah did when she cried out to God for a son. I cried out to Him, as my heart quivered with pain and anguish. I cried out for God to help me. I was so afraid to let go and trust Him and it was so hard to do. It was so easy to trust God with everything but this. Why was it so hard for me? I didn't know why, I just wanted my pain and misery to go away and not to ever worry about it again. He leaned down, pressed His face against my mine and said...

"I love you, Johnnie...I don't have a single rose to give you, but the entire field of roses...I don't have a dinner to buy for you, because I have given you the meat of my Word...I don't have a ring to give you because I have given you my Heart to have forever, if you'll receive it...Trust me...Follow me, and I will make you fishers of men..."

"You can do all things through me, who gives you the strength...You are so much stronger than you think you are..."

I finally gave my heart to Him. I gave Him the power to take control of my entire life. The years of emotional pain and rejection had devastated me. I was so consumed with finding the Knight in Shining Armor that I had made singleness my enemy. I was losing, stumbling from the plan that God had for my life. I had tried to arrange my own life and was committing emotional suicide as a result. He knew that I had gone as far as I could go. He had come to save me from myself. In my heart now, I knew it was what I needed.

I rose from my knees and wiped my face. I sat on the sofa and stared at the chair, which was now pooled with my tears.

I had now come to a place of total surrender to the Lord, not counting the cost.

As I turned my life over to Him, I finally felt peace, where there had once been constant turmoil. I wasn't going to worry about my future any more.

I finally said to the Lord, "My life in Your Hands...I will accept what you make of it."

And now began my Exodus, going forth to the Promised Land, a land that flowed with milk and honey...It was there that my destiny would be discovered.

9

Facing the Cross, Despising My Sin

∞

>...Then said Jesus unto his disciples, if any man will come after me, let him deny himself, and take up his cross, and follow me. For whosoever will save his life shall lose it; and whosoever will lose his life for my sake shall find it.
>
> Matthew 16, 24-25

My life took a radical turn after I made the decision to surrender myself totally to the Lord. I read the Bible from cover to cover, ravaging through the pages like a madman. I began to fast and pray more. I wanted to discover God's Will in every area of my life. I decided to stop dating. I wanted to devote all of my time to the Lord. I didn't know if there would ever be a Knight in Shining Armor. But the decision no longer rested on my shoulders. I left it in the hands of God.

The more time that I devoted to the Lord, the more I forgot about marriage and God's plan for my life. I spent a lot of time just talking to Him and telling Him everything that I was feeling each day. Years before I would spend most of my time praying for Him to bless me with a mate or to bless me with a job that I loved doing. Now, I was spending my time thanking Him for everything that He had done for me. I was thanking Him for waking me up in the morning. I was thanking Him for protecting me while I was at work and while I was sleeping. I began to look at life in a whole new way. I began to enjoy my life as a single person. I thanked God for blessing me to be single. I could see all of its benefits. Being single gave me time to spend with God exclusively. I didn't have to discuss my agenda for the day with anyone but Him. I didn't have to worry about what I made for dinner. Whatever it was, I would eat it and not complain. It was just a good, wholesome life and I learned to take advantage of every single day.

During the process, I fell in love with Jesus more and more each day. He was Someone that was so loving and giving. He really loved people. He loved everyone.

He was a person that always did what was right. He never compromised His standards in order to be accepted. He could speak about the Word of God because He was God. He could talk about the resurrection because He was the Resurrection. He could talk about loving His enemies because He was Love.

The power that dwelled within Him was so awesome that He could walk on water. He could stretch out His Hand and tell the raging storm to be still and the waves would just surrender in His Presence. He could simply walk up to a tomb and call death out of the body of a dead man and it would have to go.

He came to earth in the form of a human being in order to save the world. If He had not been crucified, none of us would have ever had a chance to go to Heaven. He could have chosen the easy way out and forgot about the Cross and He would have lived. But His love for mankind was greater

Facing the Cross, Despising My Sin

than the love that He had for His own Life.

I learned things that I had never heard preached on a Sunday morning about my Lord. I discovered that Jesus felt every excruciating moment of the crucifixion. He was beaten so severely that He was unrecognizable. He had been spit upon, slapped in the face, and had His beard plucked out. He was laughed at and mocked by the soldiers. He never complained once.

He was scourged, or struck with a whip that was wrapped with metal or pieces of bone. With each strike of the whip, it ripped into His flesh numerous times. Some men were rendered insane after they encountered this dreadful whipping, because of its intense pain. Even despite this, He survived. He never uttered a word.

When I was 16 years old, I was walking in my back yard and stepped on a huge nail. I could feel it ripping through my foot and just miss inches from coming out of the side of it. There is still a little hump there where that nail penetrated. It was embedded so deeply that my mom had to take a towel, and lean back on it with all the force that she could muster and pull it out. It was extremely painful to me and I was unable to walk on it for several days. But when I look back at the pain of one single nail in my foot and the pain that Jesus endured, it humbled me. It completely crippled my ability to complain about ANYTHING in my life. My complaints suddenly became meaningless.

I realized that Jesus made the ultimate sacrifice and died so that I could live. He realized the pain that He would have to bear so that everyone could have the chance to be free, and He did it anyway. I thought about my own sinfulness and self-centeredness. I thought about trivial matters that really didn't mean anything. I was complaining about not having anyone to love me when He had been there all of the time. He was on the Cross-, suffering the agony, becoming sin for someone who was saturated with it from birth. He was showing me love in a way that no human being ever could. He was suspended on the Cross; as His Beautiful Face grimaced at the ripping pain of nails in His Hands and Feet...His Heart beat against His ribcage, as sweat poured from His bloodied brow. He pressed forward to finish the job that He had been sent to do. He searched the whole time to meet His Eyes with my own, so full of love for a sinner like me.

And all that I'd ever given Him were excuses. I had become an expert at being a stubborn child...I always wanted everything to come now...Not wanting to change my plans, but wanting to do everything my way...The pain on the Cross of a Sinless Man...Yet still having the love to forgive a robber on the cross next to Him...Still having the love to see that His mother was cared for...Dying on the Cross so that He could hear me whine and complain about not having a destiny or a husband ...

I collapsed to my knees and cried in grief, ashamed of my sinful heart, a heart that did not understand what He had really done for me... I had been blinded by ignorance because I didn't understand His Sacrifice. Now I knew and it was killing me inside. There was nothing that I could do to save myself from my sinful nature and from dying in an eternal torment for the rest of my life. I couldn't save myself. I needed a Savior. I could never repay Him for what He had done for me. But all of a sudden it really became a lot easier to serve Him without question or complaint.

And so I chose to be crucified with Him. To be crucified means to give up worldly thoughts and ideas and to place our confidence in Him. It means that you forget about yourself and everything that you want. You learn to place your total trust in Him, no matter what the outcome may be. It means that you will be laughed at, and hated because He was laughed at and hated too.

I had finally come to understand that He had chosen me

to complete a task. He had chosen me before I had even born. I tried to create my future through natural means. I almost aborted my destiny in the process. I told the Lord that if He would redeem the time in my life, I would do whatever He asked me to do...

> Teach me, O Lord, the way of thy statutes; and I shall keep it unto the end...Give me understanding, and I shall keep thy law; yea, I shall observe it with my whole heart...Make me to go in the path of thy commandments; for therein do I delight...Incline my heart unto thy testimonies, and not to covetousness...Turn away mine eyes from beholding vanity; and quicken thou me in thy way...Stablish thy word unto thy servant, who is devoted to thy fear...Turn away my reproach which I fear: for thy judgments are good... Behold, I have longed after thy precepts: quicken me in thy righteousness.
> *Psalm 119:33-40*

I had spent countless hours, giving God praise for delivering me from the forces of evil. I marveled over how many times I could have ended up bound by the world and its ways. Anything could have happened to me. But God wouldn't let me go. I could never praise Him enough. I wanted God to reward me for being nice and trying to do everything just right, just the way He wanted me too. I learned that God didn't owe me anything. He didn't even owe me my life. But I owed Him everything. I was not going to get a big prize for obeying the Word of God. I was supposed to do that anyway, whether I received a blessing or not. I learned that being nice doesn't guarantee you everything you want in life. The right thing to do is to trust God for what He says is right for you. He will never be wrong. As I continued to talk with Him and read my Bible, I began to thirst for Him and was desperate to talk to Him all of the time.

I had an insatiable hunger for Him. I fought against the hours of the day. I tried to force time to expand just to have more of it to spend with Him. I rebelled against distractions and hindrances that tried to block me from reaching out to Him. I had a desire for nothing but Him day and night. I prayed for work to end to get home to Him. I fought for the weekends to devote more time to Him. There never seemed to be enough books that I could read, never enough time spent on my knees... I found myself praising Him anywhere I could for many hours at a time, losing myself in order to be closer to Him.

And for the first time in my life, it didn't matter if I got married or not. If I did get married it no longer mattered when it happened. Jesus had filled the void that had been empty in me for so long. I was happy. He had removed all of my sadness and pain. He healed every wound in my heart. He gave me tranquility in my soul. What a man...A real man...His name is Jesus.

One day, as I sat on my sofa, I told Him, "Lord, thank you for saving my life...Thank you for dying for my sins...You didn't have to do it, but you did...Thank you for caring about me. We've been together for a long time, haven't we? Even before I really knew You, You've been there for me. Thank you for loving somebody who thought she was unloved...Thank you for being there when I didn't have any friends. Thank you for being there when I walked on the playground alone, Daddy... I love you... A month later, I volunteered at an outreach in town that was started for homeless people. .

I began to approach people and talk to them. They enjoyed talking to me as much as I enjoyed talking to them. I didn't know what God was going to give me to say, but He blessed me with the words. I had the opportunity to talk to so many people. I also had the opportunity to serve them food and pray for them as well. That day, I was doing something that I really enjoyed doing. I got to talk to them about God.

I had really enjoyed the outreach and hoped that another opportunity would come like that in the near future. I felt as if a big weight had been lifted from my shoulders. I had made a small step towards the plan that God had for my life. I started to talk to anyone that would listen to me talk about the Lord. I no longer had to wait on my Knight in Shining Armor in order to talk to someone about Him. I could tell everyone on my job, everyone at home and all of my friends about Him. Over the years He had blessed me to have a variety of jobs. Each job taught me how to care about people. Some jobs taught me to communicate with people from every walk of life. Those jobs prepared me for the great plan that God had for my life. That plan was right around the corner.

10

Choosing for the Cause of Christ

∞

>...No man can serve two masters: for either he will hate the one and love the other; or else he will hold to the one, and despise the other...Ye cannot serve God and mammon.
> *Luke 16:13*

Many critics try to discredit people who have decided to be sexually abstinent by saying that God has frightened them into making that decision. They know that this is not a true statement, but only make it because nothing else seems to make any sense to them. We haven't been frightened-just enlightened.

Talking to young people in our country about abstinence is a good thing. Choosing to be abstinent until marriage gives them more time to devote to other pressing matters in life, such as college, and future endeavors. Yet there are some people who will curse you out if you even mention abstinence as if it were a fatal condition. Some parents will still tell their children to have safe sex and pray that nothing bad will happen to them. They have prophesied over their children based on the things that they may have done in their past or simply out of fear. They really don't believe that it's possible for anyone to wait until marriage to have sex.

If the sexual drive is so strong, why are some able to say no to it when given the choice? If God formed every human body from the dust of the earth, how can only a few have the discipline to say that they will wait until marriage to experience this powerful form of intimacy?

He has made it clear that He wants us to keep our bodies pure. What sense would it make for Him to leave us without the proper equipment needed to accomplish this? Of course it is impossible to resist the desires of the flesh if we aren't armed with the proper ammunition...

> There is no temptation taken you but such as is common to man: but God is faithful, who will not suffer you to be tempted above that ye are able; but will with the temptation also make a way to escape, that ye may be able to bear it.
> *I Corinthians 10:13*

We must put on the whole armor of God and stand against those things that do not represent Him. We must admit to ourselves that we are unable to control those desires on our own. Then we must pray daily for God to keep those desires under His Control until He blesses us with a mate if that is His desire. Even if it's not meant for some people to marry or remarry, He has the power to guard us from those things that hinder us and separate us from Him.

So what's the big deal? The big deal is that premarital sex is a sin. Sin causes us to slowly disintegrate our relationship with God.

I don't choose to have two masters. I have only one master and that's God. I prove my love for Him by refusing to become a slave to my flesh.

Some people will say, "It's okay to do it. You're not hurting anyone." This is their answer for doing things that they know don't line up with the Word of God. When people listen to their advice, they're nowhere to be seen when they become a victim of that advice.

No one was there with me when I was in the emergency room watching a young man who just had a "fun night out" at a club, sweating and grunting on a stretcher. His hands were tied to its sides with leather straps and police handcuffs, as he shook his balled-up fists violently. His body was full of cocaine.

Where were they when they pulled a young man out the lake after drinking all night and driving into it to his death? No one was there when a young lady tried to slash her wrists and end her life. She felt that she had nothing left to live for because her boyfriend had broken up with her.

Where were they when I stood in a hospital room and watched a young emaciated man shrivel up and die with his eyes open, with no family or friends present to tell him goodbye? He had become a victim, a life destroyed by AIDS. Was anyone there when I witnesses a teenaged girl panting and yelling out for help to ease her pain? She was giving birth to her first baby. She was 14. The father of the baby was gone. The responsibility of a child was too much for him. Suddenly, he wasn't "in love" anymore.

Nor was anyone around when I witnessed a man reaping the benefits of years of drinking. He kicked, screamed and moaned with his eyes rolled back in his head until he was dead.

You'll always hear someone say that everything is acceptable, live your life to the fullest…one snort won't kill you, one drink won't hurt you, a condom will protect you, but you never see a single one of them at the morgue. They're never at the drug and alcohol treatment centers. They're nowhere to be found. They are roaming about the earth searching for someone else to tell their lies to.

God will always be here and the Word will never fade away, no matter how much people try to eliminate it from society.

We must choose whom we will serve. Will we serve good or will we serve evil? Will we choose to be like our friends? Or will we be like our God?

Who will you serve?

11

Definition of a Miracle

∞

And a certain man was there, which had an infirmity thirty and eight years. And when Jesus saw him lie, and knew that he had been now a long time in that case, he saith unto him, Wilt thou be made whole?

The impotent man answered him, Sir, I have no man, when the water is troubled, to put me into the pool: but while I am coming, another steppeth down before me.

Jesus saith unto him, Rise, take up thy bed, and walk.

And immediately the man was made whole, and took up his bed and walked and on the same day was the Sabbath.

John 5:5-9

The miracles that I experienced daily in my life were so powerful and supernaturally mastered. The Lord certainly had His Hands all over my life in a mighty way. I would never be able to list all of the incredible miracles that God has performed in my life. If I tried, I would still be listing them thousands of years from now and just be scratching the surface. The miracle-working power of the Lord is so awesome.

One good friend that has been a great blessing in my life is Jodi Reddock. She wrote to me about her nephew Chandler ...

> When my sister was 8 weeks pregnant, she started cramping and spotting. They rushed her to the hospital and the doctor could not find a heartbeat. He told her that he didn't think that the pregnancy would last and scheduled a D and C (dilation and curettage) for the following morning. We spent the entire night believing that she had lost the baby. The next morning before the procedure, they checked one last time to attempt to find a heartbeat. Miraculously, they found the heartbeat and determined that the baby was fine. We don't know what happened the day before, but we believe that God was in complete control of the whole situation.
>
> Chandler is now almost a year old and is completely healthy and brings more joy to our lives than we ever imagined. No matter what is going on in our lives, he always makes us laugh and smile. He truly is a gift from God and I believe that he has a special purpose in life. I believe that no matter what doctors tell you, the results are ultimately up to God, the Father, the Healer, Our Lord and Savior...

I had spent most of my childhood in doctors' offices, wrestling with throat and sinus infections. I spent most of my days inside of the house. I felt so miserable. I can still

Definition of a Miracle

remember my mom insisting that I come outside to get some fresh air.

I wanted to feel better, but I didn't want to end up having my tonsils removed. So I did the only thing I could possibly do at the time...I prayed for the Lord to heal me.

I didn't think much about the prayer after I prayed it, but it was obvious that the Lord heard me. Gradually, the number of throat and sinus infections began to diminish. Eventually, the throat and sinus problems completely disappeared. I still have my tonsils. My mom was completely stunned as she saw this happening because she knew how much I suffered from those infections.

When I was growing up, I used to have a gap between my top front teeth. I didn't like it at all. I would never smile on any pictures at school because of it. I had wanted to get braces, but my parents didn't have the money to pay for them. I prayed to the Lord to make a way for us to get some money so that I could get those braces.

Unfortunately, the money didn't come, and I forgot about the prayer. Once again, God heard me, and as the years went by, when I wasn't even thinking about my teeth, He answered my prayer.

Looking at my teeth today, people always think that I had braces during some point in my life because they are very straight. But the truth is, I've never had any braces. There is no longer a gap between my front teeth. They simply grew together, through the power of God. God blessed me to have straight teeth and it didn't cost me anything, just a prayer.

Another miracle happened at work one night. I was on the elevator getting ready to return to the first floor, where I worked. I pressed the button to go down and I heard a bump, then nothing. I knew that I wasn't moving and assumed that I must be stuck on the elevator. So I called the operator on the emergency phone and told her that I was stuck. She said that she would call for someone to get me out. As I began to hear people yell above my head and receive periodic calls from the operator, I began to wonder what all the panic was about.

Eventually, some men came and pulled open the doors. I walked out it in the midst of dozens of people and a doctor. They stared at me as if they'd seen a ghost.

I discovered that that the elevator had dropped two floors! I turned around and looked behind me and couldn't believe my eyes! Light fixtures were hanging, and the entire frame of the elevator was loosened at the top and sides. Paneling from the top of the ceiling had fallen as well. And I had never heard or felt any of it! As I later talked to someone, they said that it sounded like two freight trains that had collided and could be heard as far as the sixth floor. The doctor was on the third floor checking on patients when he heard the noise and ran downstairs to see if anyone was hurt. The other nurses were screaming above me because they knew that I was the last person to get on the elevator. They were yelling to see if I was all right.

Well, I was, thanks to the Lord who grabbed the cables and held them with His Mighty Hands.

I went back to work the following day and people couldn't see how I could have walked away without a scratch. Many of them had gone to the intensive care unit to see if I was admitted. But I did walk away without a scratch.

The next miracle that occurred involved school. I finally got the opportunity to return to school and earn a Master's Degree in Practical Divinity. I was taking some correspondence classes over the Internet and began to seriously think about finishing my education. I did, except this time it was work that would help me to serve the Lord in an even greater capacity. I loved for people to ask me questions about the Bible and I enjoyed doing Biblical research. My favorite pastime was doing research on the people of the Bible and their customs during that time.

Definition of a Miracle

Next was the miracle that I had been waiting on for so long It actually happened as I sat at my desk at home, thinking. I was thinking about all of the young people in our nation and the peer pressure that they were going through in school. I would cry sometimes when I would think of some of them making the choice to become sexually active, not counting the cost of losing their virginity. They didn't understand that what they were giving away was so precious. I didn't know them at all, but my heart broke for them. There were young girls and guys out there celebrating their loss of innocence. There were young girls and guys out there in tears because they would never be able to recapture their innocence again.

"Why won't anyone tell them the truth? Why doesn't anyone care?" I cried, as I looked up into Heaven. "Why does this have to continue? Why doesn't someone do something about it?"

As I prayed, the Lord began to reveal His plan for my life. He wanted me to speak to people about abstinence and to reveal the benefits of living such a life. I honestly didn't think that such an approach had merit, because of the way that I had been received in the past. I was hesitant to talk to a group of people about this topic, because no one seemed interested in listening. But I tried anyway.

Once again, many adults that I spoke to verbally attacked me. They told me that abstinence wasn't a realistic concept. There were only a few of them that did listen and agree with me. "This won't work…It can't work…I knew they wouldn't listen to me," I said, as I paced the floor talking to God, "Why should they listen to me?"

Then I got down on my knees and prayed to Him.

"God, how can this work when no one will listen to me? I've been talking to people for over 20 years… What makes you think that they'll think differently now?" I asked in desperation.

He replied, "You're talking to the wrong people."

"What do you mean?" I asked, "Who should I be talking to, then?"

"I am going to raise up a new generation of people who will listen. I will use you to set the standard and through you many lives will be changed," He continued, "Because of your obedience to me, I will allow you to go places that you've never dreamed of going before."

Jesus said, "Follow me, and I will make you fishers of men... God blessed me to be able to go different churches and talk to teenagers about abstinence. Sometimes teenagers may only see one side of life, which is a life of sexual promiscuity. When I began to show them another side of life other than that of "following the crowd," they became eager to learn more. I suddenly felt like I had a message to offer them that would change their lives and they were ready to listen.

I was blessed to be a volunteer counselor at a variety of Christian concerts in the country. I was also blessed to help a Christian broadcasting company, as a volunteer that helped to promote Christian films. It was such a blessing to me because it allowed me the opportunity to meet so many people. And the opportunities have never lost momentum.

I now spent my time talking to young people about abstinence. I fell in love with their energy and enthusiasm for life. When I talked to them, I felt like I was a teenager all over again. So many people told me that no one would pay any attention to the abstinence message. This had been the devil's lie to begin with. It wasn't that young people didn't want to hear about it. They were dying to hear something new besides what the world had been telling them. Now God was giving it to them through someone who used to walk the playground alone when she was in grade school. She was someone who felt that she had no destiny and no purpose. She was someone who had spent a lifetime trying to find out

Definition of a Miracle

where she fit in the world. She constantly wondered why God had given her so much favor. She had felt countless tears fall at her feet from disillusionment, a broken heart and dreams. It had now been transformed into something beautiful right before her eyes. That was the reason why Satan tried so hard to destroy her before her purpose in life was fulfilled...Satan tried to abort it, but it didn't work. Now I'm out there talking to teens about abstinence, the very same subject that many adults had told me years before would never be heard by anyone. It just confirms that the Word of God will always ring true...

> But God hath chosen the foolish things of the world to confound the wise; and God hath chosen the weak things of the world to confound the things which are mighty; And base things of the world, and things which are despised, hath God chosen, yea, and things which are not, to bring to nought things that are: That no flesh should glory in his presence.
> *I Corinthians 1:27-28*

A good friend from college, Pamela Payne once wrote...

> ...God is amazing due to the wonderful, awesome things He does!!! I am so happy you are fulfilling God's purpose for your life. You wanted to be a doctor and look; you are being a doctor and helping to heal many people. You could not touch as many lives if you had been a doctor in the natural realm. In the spiritual realm, look at the number of people you are impacting. Walk in your calling and be all God has chosen you to be. No obstacles or hindrances will stand in your way because you have conquered them all. Your faith level is

greater as well as your anointing. Continue to soar higher than an eagle. It is your time!!! Be blessed and know God's got a man (kingdom man) who will treat you like a royal princess. You will be like a delicate, dainty flower in his sight...just what he is looking for. He will love you like no other natural man could possibly love you. You will be happy...all the tears, heartbreak, disappointments will be meaningless. When this man comes on the scene you will realize why an ordinary fellow was not good enough for you, virtuous woman! Don't you know how anointed you are? You can't begin to see the depth of your anointing. Take care of yourself and know God is with you. I'll keep you in my prayers...

I now have many people in my life that pray for me and give me encouragement. I have a circle of Christians that really care about and love me. Satan tried to bring bad things into my life such as sickness, heartbreak and persecution. But God used all of the bad things and brought good things to pass as a result. I used to be a person that couldn't find a friend. But the Lord blessed me to be beset with scores of people that love to hear the stories that I tell about Jesus. He has blessed me with the ability to make the pages of the Bible come alive and leap out at them with power! I love to motivate people and get them on fire about their visions and dreams. I love to pray with them and give them hope when so many people laugh at those dreams. I tell them that anything is possible with God.

I don't care how many times you took a test and failed. I don't care how many people around you are teenaged moms or how many people in your neighborhood are strung out on drugs. It doesn't matter how many times your buddies tell you to get girls pregnant or have sex with as many of them as you can. It doesn't matter if you have had sex with dozens of people over the years and now feel like you can't stop. It doesn't matter if your mom or dad abandoned you and you've had to raise yourself. Quit listening to the lies of people that try to justify society's statistics. They'll tell you that your dreams are impossible. They'll say that, according to their statistics, you'll always be sexually promiscuous. You'll always be on drugs. You'll always live in poverty. You'll be a teenaged mom just like your mother and grandmother were. They will say that you'll never finish high school.

The devil is a liar! God said that ANYTHING is possible! Never give up on your dreams.

Shallow people that claim to be representatives of God will tell you to ignore sexual abstinence. They'll tell you to just do the best you can, because you're not capable of resisting sex. You're not capable of getting free of drugs. I don't care what shape your life is in—if you drop to your knees and just ask God to come in your life and help you, He will show up and show out!

Look at all of the people that God has used mightily in the Bible. Moses had killed a man, yet God spoke to Him face to face He led the Hebrew people out of Egypt from hundreds of years of bondage by the Egyptians. Sampson had committed many sexual sins. Yet when he was at his last shred of hope, he called out to God to give him strength just one more time. His enemies had blinded him. He had turned his back on God for a season to satisfy his flesh. Only when he was blind was he able to finally see God. God heard his cry and gave him the strength to push down the massive pillars of a building and destroy his adversaries, the Philistines. At one time they held him captive and laughed at him. Now they were crushed under heaps of stone.

Paul, who was once named Saul, was someone that loathed Christians. But he was the very one that God used to spread the gospel to many lands.

So what I am saying is that nothing is impossible if you have faith and believe God. He loves you so much. You are so treasured by Him. Call out to Him today like Sampson did. Don't just sit in your condition and wander in the wilderness for 40 years like the Hebrew people did when they refused to believe God. Step out in faith and trust God. Things may not miraculously change overnight. But He'll be there with you every step of the way if you will allow Him to come into your life and change your circumstances.

12

How Bad Do You Really Want It?

∞

The same day went Jesus out of the house, and sat by the seaside. And great multitudes were gathered together unto him, so that he went into a ship, and sat; and the whole multitude stood on the shore. And he spake many things unto them in parables, saying, Behold, a sower went forth to sow; And when he sowed, some seeds fell by the wayside, and the fowls cane and devoured them up: Some fell upon stony places, where they had not much earth: and forthwith they sprung up, because they had no deepness of earth: And when the sun was up, they were scorched; and because they had no root, they withered away. And some fell among thorns; and the thorns sprung up, and choked them: And other fell into good ground, and brought forth fruit, some an hundredfold, some sixtyfold, some thirtyfold. Who hath ears to hear, let them hear.

Matthew 13:1-9

How does it work? What's the process? Is there a secret involved in choosing to remain abstinent until marriage?

Some people believe that a person who chooses to wait until marriage to have sex must be crazy, homosexual, or a super spiritual human fanatic. They don't think that type of lifestyle is normal or realistic.

We should strive to live holy. We should live a holy life daily, not when we think that we only have a few hours left to live. We should have integrity, good morals, and TOTAL respect and reverence for God. We must take care of our bodies. We should choose to do what's right instead of what's wrong. Some people find it very easy to tell lies. They don't see anything wrong with it. Some people think that it's cool to listen to derogatory music and to watch movies that are sexually suggestive. How can you see God when evil blocks your sight?

In Matthew Chapter 13, verses 1-9, I discovered the key to remaining pure until marriage…

Illustration…

Kim has listened to a message at church about abstinence. After the service is over, she leaves church, ready to go out and change the world. The abstinence message seems interesting and she makes a decision to keep her body pure until marriage. She then sees her friends at the mall. Kim tells them all about abstinence and how great it is. When her friends start to laugh at her and tell her that abstinence is not a "realistic" life to live, she immediately goes back to her old way of thinking. She listened to her friends, and like fowls of the air, they destroyed the message in an instant.

Jeff has decided to be abstinent until marriage, and for a few hours, it works. That is, until he sees his girlfriend Charlotte and thinks back to all of the passionate moments that they have spent together. He allows his flesh to decide for him and he forgets about the message. His flesh has scorched the words and they've just become a fading memory for him. What really matters now is "the moment".

Allison will listen to the message, and then apply it to her life for a period of time. Then she turns 28 and sees her all of her friends getting married by trying "Plan B" which is premarital sex. She then starts to "think" and tells herself that perhaps "Plan B" isn't that bad after all. She has no faith in the outcome of her situation. The thorns represent what she sees her friends with that she can't have fast enough and she becomes discouraged. The thorns wrap around the message and choke it to death.

Bradley, on the other hand, has received the message and made a commitment to stand on the Word of God until he gets his blessing. He transmits the message to everyone he knows. He speaks to his friends and when they laugh at him, he speaks even more fervently. He tells his children when he is married and then his children tell their children and the seed grows and multiplies and is not destroyed because it is now in good soil.

When someone says that they have made a commitment to be sexually abstinent, critics will laugh and say that the person is homosexual. Why? Because they operate from their flesh and their heart has become hardened. Once a person has hardened their heart to the Word of God, everything becomes acceptable to them. It's as if they have a dark cloud that shadows His Word, making it difficult for them to see the truth.

What made the process work for me is the spiritual intimacy that I have with God. It is something that's so deep and awesome. It's something that's so intimate that its power is greater than anything I've ever experienced. My very life, body, and soul are placed on the altar before the Lord. I love Him so deeply that I refuse to let any human take His place whether I am single or married. He can't be replaced because He is a jealous God and will not stand side by side with anyone! Even if He had to personally reach down from Heaven and remove that idol, He will not be #2 in my life.

Anything that I know is not pleasing to Him I choose not to participate in. I will not allow my flesh to dominate my relationship with Him. My relationship with Him is one that is Spirit to Spirit. My flesh has no place in this relationship. Excuses will not work in this relationship. It's one that's all about yielding to God's Will and not my own. It's a relationship that allows me to be naked in my heart and spirit and not be ashamed. I don't have to give anything to Him to prove my love to Him except my heart. It's a moment where I pour out all of the words that are in my heart and allow them to weep on His Shoulders in open humility.

Some people can't understand what I feel for Him, but the only thing that matters is that He understands. He loves and accepts me just as I am, complete with flaws and shortcomings. Isn't it so wonderful that He will accept us just as we are?

When my mind becomes swamped with all of the filthy language and stories at work, and the negative reports from critics, I pray to ward those things from my mind.

In the end, the process worked for me because I loved the Lord more than myself. The secret in choosing to be abstinent until marriage and making it stick is choice. It simply comes down to choice. We choose…God gives everyone the ability to chose. He will not stop us from doing what we want to do. We choose to practice sexual abstinence, and it's not as impossible as some people say that it is. It's very possible. Some people have chosen to ignore it, and then become angry with others that embrace it. There is no magic bullet that makes one person more capable than another. We are all created by the Hands of God. The strength is embedded in the relationship we have with the Lord. This gives us the capability to make the choice.

Do you desire to be like everyone else, or do you desire to

be obedient to God in every area of your life? If you really desire God, then you will work hard to strengthen areas that you are weak in with daily prayer and the Word of God. But some people will allow peer pressure to make the choice for them.

Quit worrying about what people think! Peer pressure is nothing but Satan bullying the children of God into becoming a servant of sin. God wants people that don't care what others think about them. He wants people who will choose to serve Him instead of their flesh. The big picture is getting to Heaven, not pleasing a human being that has no possible way of getting you there.

Benefits of Sexual Purity

1. Freedom from sexually transmitted diseases.
2. Freedom from pregnancy.
3. Freedom from worrying about going to the doctor for contraceptives and being tested for a sexually transmitted disease.
4. Freedom from being stressed emotionally because of #1, #2, and #3.
5. Freedom to focus on the Lord.
6. Freedom to focus on school and the future.
7. Freedom to trust God for your mate and not have to rely on becoming sexually active in order to get one.
8. Freedom to be thoroughly excited that you waited until your wedding night to experience sexual intimacy with your new husband/wife!
9. Freedom to realize that by committing your life to God, you have really made Him smile!
10. Freedom to know in your heart that you are not a servant to sin, but that you are free!

**Benefits of Being Sexually Active
Without Marriage**

NONE

13

Is It Worth the Wait?

∞

> Again, the kingdom of heaven is like unto a merchant man, seeking goodly pearls: Who, when he had found one pearl of great price, went and sold all that he had, and bought it.
> *Matthew Ch. 13: 44-46*

I peeked through the store window at the wedding dresses as I usually did on many Saturday mornings. I watched the sales clerk bring the dresses out, fluffing them and making sure that they were just perfect for display. The crisp folds of white satin glistened on the mannequin, anticipating the arrival of a young lady that would gasp at its sight and grab hold of it. Many young girls have dreamed of the day when they would get to walk down the aisle in a beautiful wedding dress, smiling in front of a crowd, so happy and in love.

I had peered through that same window for many years, wondering if it would ever be my turn or whether I was ever meant to have a turn. I often wondered as I watched all of my college buddies get married and slowly fade away into the sunset, smiling as I waved them goodbye.

One of the most common prayers that we hear today from singles is the prayer for God to bless them with a mate. Those who are single have heard all of the same familiar lines such as "Just wait and God will send you somebody", "What do you want to get married for?" "You're better off by yourself" and the classic, "They're on the way, just hold on a little longer."

Some married couples will tell someone that's single "What do you want to get married for?" They may say this in order to make the single person think twice about getting married as if it were a contagious disease that they didn't want them to catch. Others will say, "I wouldn't change one single thing...I love being married," as if they were missing out on life's greatest treasure if they didn't get married. Then they end up so confused, they don't know what to ask God for. If marriage is so terrible, why did God create it? If marriage is so great, then why am I still single?

To say that God has somebody for everybody is not true because there are some people that will never get married, because perhaps God has another plan for their lives that would be hindered if they were married. Sometimes married people say this like an old broken record, trying to encourage a singles person that it will happen one day, when in fact it may not if it is not the Will of God.

When God places two people together, they form a team that works in some capacity through that marriage to bring Him glory. Some people are in marriages that are not very happy at all. They will tell a person that's single not to ever get married because their marriage is in disarray. Other people will say that marriage is beautiful, because their marriage has harmony and will encourage a single person to get married.

What about the people that don't get married? Sometimes married couples don't like discussing this option because they don't want to let the single person down or discourage their dreams. There are some people that do want to get married and will not get married because of bad choices. They have spent most of their lives chasing after people that were never right for them in the first place. Some people waste their lives lamenting because they don't have a mate. They sit at home waiting for them to come and knock on their door instead of getting out of the house and working as servants of the Lord diligently until He decides to bring that person into their path.

If it's not God's Will for you to be married, He will place a peace within you that will confirm it. If it is His Will for you to be married and you've hit the age of 30 and haven't seen it happen yet, don't have a stroke. You must be patient and allow the Lord to bring that person into your life, not by sitting at home and crying about it, but by becoming so busy and preoccupied with the things of God that you will find yourself at a place where the thought of marriage doesn't consume your mind daily.

There are some people that will tell you that you will never be married because you have chosen to be abstinent until marriage. If you don't get married and you have been obedient to God, don't think that it was because of your stand. It was because God decided that He didn't feel that it was best for your life. Sometimes the greatest blessings come when we give the biggest sacrifices, when we lay those things that seem to mean the most to some people at the Feet of the Lord.

You can be sure that if it's His Will for your life to be married that the blessing will be so big that it will be beyond words...

I have often tried to picture what it would be like to be married and imagine what type of person he would be. What would it be like to actually get to cook for a guy, to look into his eyes and smile lovingly as we cover our feet in sand and we relaxed on the beach? I've often tried to imagine actually having someone drive for me, or to just hear someone say, "I love you" for no particular reason, or just to get a two week honeymoon... The greatest thrill for me would be to actually have a nice, elegant, candlelight dinner with someone that actually has something in common with me...Love for the Lord!

He too, would have spent his whole life looking for a godly woman. Not just an average woman, but a woman that was unusual and extraordinary. He would look for her just like a fisherman who was searching for one pearl in particular. He would look and pray as he searched through his fisher's net. Every now and then he would see a beautiful shiny pearl and ask, "Is it her?"

And the Lord would say, "No son, it's not."

He would sit at home watching television one evening and see a commercial about a tropical island resort. He would wonder what it would be like to go there for a honeymoon with the wife that he had been praying for. He would get on his knees and ask "Lord when will it be my time?"

And the Lord would say, "Not yet, son."

Sometimes he would look in the mirror in the morning as he would get dressed for work, and notice another gray hair at his temple and he would sigh and wonder, "Lord, how long?"

And the Lord would say, "Not long, son."

One day he would stand on the porch of the house that he bought to share with the wife that he had been praying for. He would look out over the sunset and wonder, "When is it time, Lord?"

And the Lord would say, "Trust me, son." One day he decides to lay down his fisher's net. It seems so empty, even though it's full of beautiful pearls. Suddenly, he sees one that is at the very bottom of the net. It's not as beautiful as the other pearls, yet it glistens as bright as the sun. He looks up towards heaven, and the Lord, says, "Now, son." He would reach out happily, eagerly, and full of joy and take that pearl into his arms. That pearl would be me.

He would make me his wife. He would choose me over every woman in the world because, in his sight, I was a pearl of a great price.

I would like to be married one day. I hope that it's God's Will for my life. What do I do, then, if it's not His Will?

It would be great to have a godly husband that I could grow old with... I would love to experience childbirth (minus the pain) and have someone to massage my feet at the end of a long day. I would love to have him place rose petals on our bed on our honeymoon night. I'd love for him to sing love songs to me (all of romantic stuff that I've always dreamed of.)

What would be the worst thing that would happen if I never got married? What would I have at the end of my life if I never made it to the altar? The answer is I would have what I had when I first came into the world....

Jesus.

Forever.

If I never get married, I will have the thrill of knowing that Jesus will be my Groom His love for me is so powerful, so refreshing to my soul that words can't describe it. What would it be like to have a dance with Jesus? What does it feel like to be His bride? I would put on my finest attire, decorate my home and fill it with the most expensive perfumes that money could buy. I would fill it with beautiful roses and anoint the house in every corner of every room. I would call the angels in to play beautiful music on their harps as I waited for Him to enter the room.

As He walked into the room, I would find myself humbled by His Sinless Presence and Awesome Aroma. I would feel so filthy, even in my garments of white, in comparison to His Holiness and Purity. I would be too ashamed to ask for a dance, although my heart would beat for it just the same. As I would fall to my knees in humiliation and shame, He would scoop me up with His Mercy and Grace. He would smile and tell me how much He loved me. He would tell me that I was the apple of His Eye.

As the music would play in the background, He would hold out one nail-scarred Hand and say, "May I have this dance?"

Tears would stream down my face, as my trembling hand would take His. He would lead me in the dance, as a groom that danced proudly with His bride. He would laugh and dance with me all around the room as the light of His Glory radiated in timeless space. I would stare at Him in awe, completely mesmerized by His love for me... What love, what passion, what a Man...A real Man...

His name is Jesus.

14

Behold...A Handmaiden of the Lord!

∞

> ...And he beheld them and said, What is this that is written, the stone which the builders rejected, the same is become the head of the corner? Whomsoever shall fall upon that stone shall be broken, but on whomsoever it shall fall, it will grind him to powder.
> *St. Luke, 20:17-18*

I think that the number one question that is asked by teenagers today is "Why should we wait until marriage to have sex?" They may have watched movies and television programs that promote sexual promiscuity in a positive light openly and freely. The characters portrayed seem to be so happy and carefree.

But in retrospect, everything that you see doesn't always represent what really is. When teens and adults have asked about abstinence, there are actually few that don't want to hear about it. They really want to know more about it and more importantly, why no one's ever told them about it.

Some parents will not tell their teens about abstinence. If they have had sex before marriage they may think that it will also be hard for their teens to wait.

Parents, it is imperative that that you tell your children about abstinence until marriage, whether they decide to make that choice or not. You may be surprised at the decision that they may make in the long run because of the seed that you plant in their mind. Don't take this choice away from them by being silent.

There are a few reasons why we shouldn't have sex until marriage. The first reason is that this was something that was sanctioned by God in the first place. We, as carnal and sinful human beings dropped the ball thousands of years ago after Adam and Eve committed the first sin. We took something that was supposed to be passionately shared between a husband and his wife and mutilated it, attempting to make it void of any beauty at all. It has no longer become the blessing of a marital union but has become an expected convenience between two parties that seek an instant gratification without having to exercise patience.

Now we are faced with scores of sexually transmitted diseases, some of which have no cure, such as herpes and AIDS, and many people who are now suffering from the consequences of listening to human knowledge instead of Perfect Knowledge that comes from God.

It's a good feeling to go through life without having extra pressures. When you are sexually active, you may worry about having sexually transmitted diseases, and AIDS. You may worry about becoming pregnant. I have learned that it's a blessing not to have to worry about these issues. I can devote my time to other issues in my day instead of having tests done for sexually transmitted diseases. I don't have to pay for medications for those diseases. God wants us to spend our time worshipping and doing work for Him. These issues do not promote the glory for Him, but instead bring

Behold...A Handmaiden of the Lord!

glory to Satan.

Another reason, and to me, the greatest reason to wait until marriage to have sex is because of the love of Jesus. It presses against my conscience to deliberately commit sin in this manner because He gave His Life so that I could have a chance at eternal life. I know that sex must be an extremely powerful force. It has created havoc in the lives of mankind for centuries. It has caused brother to kill brother, and husband to kill wife. It has caused people to go emotionally insane. They could not cope with the separation of someone they loved when that person broke up with them in a sexual relationship. It has caused consciences to die for a single moment because of its ultimate pleasure.

Another reason to remain abstinent is that the memories of sexual unions with people in past relationships will be etched in your memory forever. Satan will see the memories of all of your sexual experiences and take pictures of them. He keeps the roll of film in his hand at all times and tries to use it against you. He threatens you with dreams and memories of those people that you try to put behind you. Even though you have asked God to forgive you and He has, Satan will always try to hold that roll of film over you. He will say that God hasn't forgiven you.

When you ask Jesus to forgive you for those sexual sins, He WILL forgive you. The memories will remain in your mind forever. But He will do something different with that film. He will take it and rip it out of its container. When He does this, and it's exposed to the light, the contents on the film are destroyed forever. This means that when Jesus forgives you, He never remembers your sin again.

Now I'll talk about rejection. When we choose to remain sexually pure until marriage, we are guaranteed to encounter some form of rejection. It may be from friends, family, or associates. With that in mind, we must understand that Jesus, who is Perfect and Sinless, was too rejected because of His unwillingness to follow the world…

> …He is despised and rejected of men; a man of sorrows and acquainted with grief as it were our faces from him; he was despised and we esteemed him not.
>
> *Isaiah, 53:2-3*

One of the greatest obstacles that I have had to face and overcome is rejection. It is something that can be hard to understand if you are the recipient of it. Jesus was the Promised Messiah. But He was still rejected by people in His own community. He was even betrayed by His own disciple, Judas. But He still managed to keep His focus on the mission that He had been sent to accomplish. He chose not to listen to the critics.

During my own lifetime I have faced rejection by people that I thought were good friends. But when it came to really understanding who I was and what I stood for, they didn't have a clue. They were unable to understand my thoughts and actions and why I was so focused on Jesus. They couldn't understand why I had no desire to do certain things and act a certain way.

They couldn't understand why I wouldn't just settle for any guy. They couldn't understand why I refused to live like the world. I had faith that so many of my dreams would come true one day. Because it seemed like my dreams were so out of the ordinary and my life so out of the ordinary, many people wrote me off as nonsensical.

But who could love Jesus so much that they would sacrifice all of the pleasures of life, including sex, marriage, and children, and choose to wait on the timing of God? Who would choose to dream big and believe that anything was possible with God?

I could.

Is it Worth the Wait?

I have also been criticized for attending a multi-racial church. I was told that I had "alienated" my race by diversifying with Christians of different cultures. Where is it written that Jesus taught anyone to separate from certain people because of the shade of their skin?

The Bible says that we should abhor sin. I abhor racism. Jesus doesn't condone racism. But many people do...

If a man say, I love God, and hateth his brother, he is a liar: for he that loveth not his brother whom he hath seen, how can he love God, whom he hath not seen? I John 4:20

I have also faced rejection because of my appearance. Some people have told me that I was unattractive. No matter what I did, no matter how much makeup I put on or what outfit I wore, there were people out there that teased me because of the way I looked.

I spent many nights praying to God to make me beautiful. If I could just be beautiful, I could be accepted then, I thought.

But God would say to me, "Johnnie, I sat down and created your face with my Own Hands...I would look at the flowers outside and say, "She is even more beautiful than every flower I have ever formed. I would mold your nose and smooth over your eyes and say to myself, "She is so wondrously created in my Own Image." I would look down and smile at you as I shaped your lips to be so lovely because I knew that one day I would hear my Own Words come back and speak to me. You are so beautiful to me, my angel. There isn't any man on the face of the earth that I could ever give you, that will ever understand how truly beautiful you are...I made you just the way you are, because you have been manufactured and molded by My Hands...

I never prayed for God to make me beautiful again.

I write these words so that you will know that when bad things happen to God's children, He will always bring a good thing out of it. Even though I suffered rejection from some people, God took that rejection and blessed me to meet people from other nationalities and from many walks of life that accepted me as I was, no strings attached. By meeting new people, I opened up a way for them to get to know another race of people based on the good fruit that He had placed in me.

God brought other people into my life that saw me as a beautiful treasure and as someone to behold and cherish. They were able to listen to my heart and could see beauty on the inside that exuded to the outside. Where I was once shunned by some men and constantly picked on by many of my peers, I have pictures taken of me all of the time. I used to be too shy to get in front of a camera. Now it's a lot of fun.

I have been blessed to meet some of the most prominent people in the Christian entertainment industry and in the world. They were opportunities that God blessed me to have. I never imagined that I would meet all of the people that I have met in my life. But God did promise me that He would take me places that I had never been.

It is through the painful times that we gain our strength and ability to weather any storm through His Power. When He blesses us, it is always something that's beyond our wildest dreams. Because I have faced rejection and overcame it through the Word of God, I can tell other people about my life and how God can mend wounds and broken hearts and restore days that have been robbed by the enemy. I now have a blessing of friends from all four corners of the world. I got them by being open and loving all people, not by closing myself off to one certain race of people. None of this would have happened without God.

I write this testimony to all of the young people that have been hurt by rejection. I know what it feels like to be called names and to be excluded from groups. I know what it feels like to lie in bed and cry all night long because you think something is wrong with you because you don't seem to fit in anywhere. I know what it feels like to be called names like crazy, stupid, and a nerd. I know what it feels like to be constantly abandoned by people that claim to love you. I also know what it feels like to be betrayed by someone that says that they'll be there for you forever. I am able to say in this season of my life...

> ...From henceforth let no man trouble me: for I bear in my body the marks of the Lord Jesus. I say today that is has been an honor to endure such a light affliction for the cause of Christ.

There are some of you that are seconds short of having a nervous breakdown. Because of the sexual experiences that torment you...the heart that has been broken repeatedly and never seems to heal...Because it feels so unloved. There are some of you that are just seconds away from giving in to sex... Because you want to be loved so badly by someone...by anyone. Some of you have cried so many nights until you feel that God has forgotten about you. You have made a commitment to remain pure until marriage and nothing seems to be coming your way in the form of a blessing, only loneliness it seems.

I want you to know that there is hope and it is in Jesus. If you place your trust in Him totally and have patience, blessings will rain from heaven. When you feel those feelings of hopelessness rage in your body, kneel down before the Lord and tell Him your whole heart. When the desire flashes before your eyes to return to a life of sexual promiscuity, when you feel like giving up on sexual abstinence, kneel down before the Lord and ask Him to help you with weakness of the flesh. He is the only one with the power to help you sustain and stay encouraged. Stay in the Word of God and never give up. He will transform your life in ways that you could never imagine.

Stone the Builders Rejected

Who is the stone the builder's rejected, you ask? It is Jesus. He was the Stone that many men said was not the Son of God. He was repeatedly rejected for being exactly who He said He was. He is now the Head, because of His sacrifice for the lives of mankind. His Name will reign forever and it will never be erased from the earth, no matter how people try to dismiss Him and say that He doesn't exist.

Who is the stone the builder's rejected? I was a stone that the builders rejected because I chose to be different. It is everyone that has made a commitment to remain abstinent until marriage. You will be rejected as Jesus was because we are followers of His Footsteps and refuse to follow the ways of the world. We are the head and not the tail because we have made a decision to remain steadfast to the cause, all the way, to the end of our last breath. We love Him that much.

I was rejected because of my commitment to Jesus Christ. It has caused me great pain at times, but I chose to remain faithful to the words of the Lord because they couldn't be wrong. The Bible says, Heaven and earth shall pass away, but my words will never pass away. Stick to your committment and wait on the Lord. He will never fail you, nor will His Word. The Word will never lose its power.

Hold on to your faith, and never let it die. Jesus told Peter, "Peter, the devil has desired to have you that he may sift you as wheat, but I have prayed for thee, that thy faith fail not."

No matter what you go through on this journey, no matter how much you are laughed at or criticized, never lose your faith. If you lose your faith, you have lost the war. Draw nigh to the Lord and He will draw nigh to you.

Who shall fall on the stone and be broken? It will be others that you have the opportunity to witness to about your life. Your words might be the very ones that will cause them to humble themselves and be broken for the cause of Christ.

Who shall the stone fall upon and crush into powder? It will be those very ones that have tried to crush the children of God by attempting to lance them with their pessimism and negative statements.

Dare to be the stone the builders rejected. When you do, you too will be the head of the corner, broken perhaps, bloodied, perhaps, but blessed of God, even better than you could ever imagine...

Virginity is a precious gift from God. Cherish it and do not allow anyone to manipulate you into giving it away for free. It's costly. It's like the most expensive diamond in the world. It's too precious to throw away. Never let go of it until you get married. You'll be glad you did. I have now walked with the Lord for 37 years... I continue to talk to young people about abstinence. God has blessed me greatly. Now I honor Him by allowing the Word of God to spring forth from my lips in order to motivate and encourage them. His Word will give birth to a new generation of people that will listen and concur. My eyes have not become faded and dim to the promises that He has yet to bless me with one day...We have been together all of these years, Side by side, Hand in hand...And the best is yet to come...

And there He walks cheerfully down the road as the sand skips under His sandals. A trickle of sweat gleams on His cheek and disappears into His Beard. A soothing breeze brushes His Hair back lightly on His Forehead. His garment sways gently and peacefully as He walks. Even the trees smile and clap their hands as He passes by, as His Sweet Aroma penetrates their nostrils. He finally stops by the seashore. He stoops down and picks up one of the nets that belongs to a fisherman and holds it out to you ...

He says, "Follow me and I will make you a fisher of men..."

I did....What about you?

Make the decision today not to conform to the world but to be transformed by the renewing of your mind. Look to please God and not man. Choose life...choose abstinence

Magnify the Lord today... Tomorrow... and Forever...The grace of our Lord Jesus Christ be with you. My love be with you all in Christ Jesus. Amen.

To contact Ms. Goolsby, e-mail her at
http://instrumentsofgod.homestead.com
Purest Temple Ministries
347 College St.#2-I
Macon, Ga.31201

Notes

Notes

Printed in the United States
937100002B